EB

To Lyndl:

Could not have done
it without you.
Really!
If you read it again,
and you find something,
please don't tell me.
We made it!

Bert

A boy...a family...
a neighborhood...
and a lost civilization...
memories of growing up
in Brooklyn NY
in the '40s and '50s

By Bert Kemp

Published by Paerdegat Park Publishing, Box 798, Darien, CT 06820

Printed in the United States of America

Cover design by the author

Publishers Cataloging-in-Publication Data
Kemp, Bert
EB : a boy--a family--a neighborhood--and a lost civilization--memories of grow-
ing up in Brooklyn, New York in the '40s and '50s.
Bert Kemp. --1st ed.
p. cm
EB is nickname of protagonist.

1. Kemp, Bert--Childhood and youth. 2. Brooklyn (New York, N.Y.)--Biography.
3. Brooklyn (New York, N.Y.)--Social life and customs. I Title.

F129.B7K46 1998 974.7'23043'092 [B]   QBI98-738

Library of Congress Catalog Card Number: 98-66008

ISBN 0-9663803-0-4

0 9 8 7 6 5 4 3 2 1

First Edition

Paerdegat Park Publishing

Dedication

To my wife Cindy, who prodded and pushed, and when that didn't work, cajoled and flattered me into getting down to work. And then cheered me on by smiling and laughing, sighing and crying, or otherwise reacting to each day's work as if it were written by a Hemingway...or a Faulkner.

Instead of a Kemp.

To my children, James, William, Elizabeth, and Victoria, who had absolutely nothing to do with the writing of this book. But who did their job by growing up to be very nice people who are a pleasure to be with at all times. I'm very proud of them for that accomplishment.

To my grandchildren, Callum James and Kathryn Rose, who are off to a very good start in following in the footsteps of their aunt and uncles.

To Dottie, who helped (and continues to help) in more ways than are countable.

To all my friends from Brooklyn whose story this is. The ones who are named and the ones who are not. Especially Bud Bohan and Jerry Frost, who helped with research and provided important information and detail.

And finally, to Brooklyn, New York, the real hero of this story. To all of you out there who did not grow up in Brooklyn, I mean no disrespect when I say that I cannot conceive of a better place to have spent my early life. The Golden Age is gone now, but to all those who were there and lived through it with me, this is my way of saying...I remember.

And I loved every minute of it, too.

To the Reader

On one level, this is an old fashioned book.

Because it's about honor, integrity, self-reliance, friend-ship, independence, personal responsibility, religion, patriotism, self-sacrifice, honesty, fairness, and mutual respect.

And love.

On a second level, this is a new fashioned book.

Because it's about vacillation and tenacity, obstinacy and lack of commitment, conformity and contrariety, Catholicism and skepticism, traditionalism and iconoclasm, success and failure.

And yes, love.

But levels notwithstanding, this is simply a book about a time and a place. A wonderful place of neighborhoods and parishes and consistency and constancy; a place of well-used front stoops, second-home candy stores and club-like saloons; a place of time-honored values and life-long friendships; a contrarily sophisticated but endearingly innocent place; a woefully misunderstood place; the biggest small town in America... Brooklyn, New York.

At a magical moment in time...the 1940s and '50s.
The Golden Age.

But most of all, this is a book about kids...kids before television...and how they ate and slept in their homes but lived their lives on the streets and in the neighborhoods, how they lived with their neighbors not just among them, and how they created, organized, and presided over one of the most unique, complex, and self-regulating subcultures of all time. And how they did all that without an adult in sight.

It's a book about special kids.

Brooklyn kids.

And everything in this book is true.

All the places are real. All the people are real. All the names are their own. All the stories, all the vignettes, all the escapades are true. But, of course, I tweaked a little here, embellished a bit there, romanticized a bit here, and dramatized a little there. That's my job. So please cut me some slack on the details. Chalk it up to poetic license.

And speaking of truth, I did a few other things, too.

I changed some names, especially several of the girls, because I didn't want to embarrass anyone.

I played with some dates and times and guessed at some ages. If I'm not exactly right, I'm close. In a few of the vignettes, I substituted some of the peripheral people to keep the cast of characters to a manageable number.

Obviously, I couldn't vouch for the accuracy of much of the dialogue (nobody's memory is that good), so I presented all conversation in upper case as a visual reminder that I'm doing some guessing. In those cases where the dialogue is central to the story, the words are right on and accurate, or as close as I could get. In all cases, I tried to be true to my own and other people's memories of each and every scene.

In addition, I will admit to giving EB the best of it where I could. His weaknesses and warts are certainly there, and nothing is stretched beyond the truth, but I will agree that at certain times he comes off as slightly larger than life.

Deliberately.

For the purposes of this book, I see EB as more than a literal, real person. He is also emblematic of his time...a creature of his age. In the '40s and '50s, we grew up on hyper-muscled superheroes in the comic books; mysterious defenders of truth, justice, and the American way on the radio; and World War II propaganda films in the movies. And lived our lives with those images firmly (and always) in our heads. Given the right circumstance, EB acted as if he were (and probably believed himself to be) Jack Armstrong-the All American Boy, Batman, The Flash, The Shadow, or Captain Marvel.

We all did.

We believed in heroes...we created them...believed in them...and insisted that they be mythical.

And so they were.

And in our hearts, so were we.

And finally, in the spirit of this confessional, I should also acknowledge a slight admiration for EB.

And a modicum of affection.

Bert Kemp, 1998

EB was a wiseguy.

No, not a Mafia kind of wiseguy. A Brooklyn kind of wiseguy.

Big difference.

EB was full of himself, sure of himself (most of the time), arrogant, a ball buster, a clubhouse lawyer.

With a twinkle.

The twinkle was the difference. Without the twinkle, he would have been just a clichéd New York kind of wiseguy. Decidedly not attractive. The twinkle defined EB as a '40s-'50s kid from Brooklyn.

The twinkle made EB who he was.

The twinkle was his salvation. The subtle ones saw it, recognized it, fell for it. He drove them nuts, but they loved him in spite of themselves.

The others didn't matter to EB.

But EB was definitely an acquired taste.

One day in early summer, Gilbert Hefner's family decided to build a fish pond in the backyard. Naturally, they didn't pay a contractor to come and dig it out. The older boys of the block did the work. In the '40s and '50s, nobody paid out money except when absolutely necessary. The people of EB's neighborhood were comfortable but certainly not rich. The only thing they were rich in was kids. There were always plenty of kids around so they were put to work whenever possible probably for nothing more than cold Cokes and lemonade.

EB was about four years old when the Hefners decided to go ahead with the project. He was always attracted to anything unusual happening on his block, and since the Hefner house was only a few doors away, this was an irresistible magnet for EB.

He hung around. He wouldn't go away. He got in the way. He chattered. He asked dumb questions...HEY GUYS, WATCHA DOIN', HUH?...WHAT'S THE HOLE FOR?...WOW, IT'S REALLY DEEP, HUH GUYS?...GONNA BE A POOL?...CAN I SWIM IN IT?...HEY, WILL SOMEONE TEACH ME HOW TO SWIM?...WILL YA?...WILL YA, BOB?...WILL YA, GILLY?... HUH?...IT'S FOR FISH?...BOY, THAT'S DUMB...WHAT KIND OF FISH?...BIG FISH, LOOKS LIKE...HOW BIG?...BIGGER 'N ME?...HEY, I'M PRETTY BIG...DO FISH COME THIS BIG?...

He wouldn't shut up.

As the hole got deeper, approaching five feet, EB wanted to be down there, at the bottom of that magnificent, mysterious pit. He voiced that desire, over and over. And the older boys were not happy with his high decibel chirps. The diggers were definitely not digging him at that moment.

One of the big boys that day was Bob Campbell, EB's older cousin who lived with him three doors away at 791 East 40th Street. Bob was seven years older than EB and had a bit of a twinkle himself. (Maybe it was in the genes.)

SO YOU WANT TO BE DOWN THERE...said Bob...OK, WE'LL LET YOU GO DOWN THERE, RIGHT GUYS?...And they lowered EB down into that fresh, soft, sweet smelling, caressing crater.

As he descended EB couldn't stop smiling and chattering. He was thrilled.

But he was four years old, and after only about five minutes or so of exploration, he was bored. So he started to scream to be let out of that rotten, stinking hole.

Scream.

Silence.

Scream. Louder.

Silence.

The boys were gone. They simply up and walked away and left him down there in that frightening grave-like hole.

Alone.

Unforgivably, they were gone...but not too far. They were enjoying a leisurely lunch in the Hefner kitchen. They heard him of course but they were on their lunch break.

Union guys.

EB settled down. He knew somebody would save him. Somebody always did. In this neighborhood, everybody knew everything. Especially the mothers. Mothers knew all. They had a very efficient communication system.

Ten minutes later, EB's mother was at the Hefner house, and eleven minutes later, the boys were retrieving EB from that hateful hole.

All the boys suffered in various ways for their unforgivable, callous act toward this cute little boy who was practically still a baby. But it was tougher on EB's cousin.

Bob Campbell lived on the second floor of EB's house with his brother John, their father Rob (Uncle Rob), and their grandmother (EB's grandmother, too). There was no mother. Martha Campbell had died soon after John was born.

So EB's mother was the acting mom for Bob and John.

That's why it was worse for Bob. As acting mom, she acted decisively and physically. When it came to discipline, EB's mom was old school. She no doubt gave Bob a few whacks on the behind with the dreaded "green stick", the one she kept in the broom closet, the one that EB would know so well later on.

Quick, efficient, frontier justice.

As for EB, he knew the guys would get him out of the hole. He was calm and cool with the whole thing. He was a Brooklyn kid, and as early as age four he had an instinct for the code of the street. When the older boys teased him and roughed him up like that, he knew they loved him.

And Bob Campbell was more than an older cousin to EB. He was an idol, a mentor, a father figure.

And God knows, EB needed that.

EB's father was a warm, physically expressive man with soft, unwavering hazel eyes that always told you exactly how much he loved you.

That's how he was when he was himself.

But all too often he wasn't himself.

Then he was someone else. Then Dr. Jeykell became Mr. Hyde. Then he was an angry, abusive alcoholic and a sometime irresponsible gambler. On any given night, EB and his family didn't know whether they would have a father and a husband or a mind-altered monster. Whether they would spend the rest of that night happy or sad, smiling or crying. Or, if he was on a gambling binge, whether they would have any money for food.

Hard times.

If EB's dad came directly home from work, he arrived at exactly five forty-five. So EB, his mother, and his little sister Dorothy started worrying at five thirty-five. As the clock ticked slowly (slow motion minutes really do exist and they are surely the devil's creation), their anxiety grew. His mother busied herself in the kitchen; the kids were usually in the living room on the floor pretending to be finishing homework or reading a comic book. They never said a word to each other, but by a quarter to six, they were emotional wrecks. If they heard the front door open, the kids let out a deep breath, smiled at each other, waited for kisses, hugs, the evening paper, and pieces of Wrigley's Juicy-Fruit chewing gum. Daddy was home.

But if they didn't hear the opening door at five forty-five their hearts sank. Trouble.

How much trouble depended on how late he was. The later he was, the drunker he was.

It was an equation.

When he finally appeared, the transformation was amazing. The warmth and the caring were replaced by cold, hard eyes, unrelenting anger, and threatened physical harm in the form of false charges and raised-fist feints like some kind of jungle animal. And all of that directed not at the kids but at their mother or the world in general. There was screaming from both, mild cursing from him, and from her, occasionally going over the edge, a whack on his head with a cooking pot.

Sad.

EB's father was a diminutive man, lean and sinewy. He worked very hard, physically hard, in the repair shops of the New York City Fire Department. He worked six days a week, but all that hard labor provided very little money for his family. Whether that contributed to his drinking problem, nobody would ever know. In the '40s, people did not have the time nor the luxury of sitting around in armchairs and psychoanalyzing themselves. EB's father was too busy coping with his life to stop and try to figure it all out.

But on the other hand, EB's father's life could be described as a psychiatrist's fantasy.

Textbook stuff.

His mother and father were killed in a train accident when he was nine years old. Terrible enough. But to make it an honest-to-God tragedy, his older sister was taken in by relatives while he was put into St. John's Home for Boys. St. John's was located in Rockaway Beach, of all places. He stayed there for almost two years before he was rescued by his uncle, his mother's brother. The uncle, who was very fond of him, finally retrieved him from the orphanage, took him in, and tried to treat him as his own son.

But the uncle's real son, who was about the same age as EB's father, had a big problem with that. Evidently they lived in a small house with only two bedrooms. That meant the son had to share his parents, his room and his bed with EB's father. And he surely whined and complained about the unfairness of it all to his very sympathetic mother.

Who eventually had a big problem with it, too.

She waited for eight or nine months, and while her husband was out of town on a business trip, she asked EB's father if he wanted to take a ride out to the Rockaways to see his old friends at St. John's Home for Boys.

Well, sure...that would be nice, he probably thought to himself.

He could go back to the home and do some bragging among the orphans. He had a family now. Sure, why not.

When they rang the front doorbell of St. John's and the Mother Superior answered the door, she showed not the least surprise. But EB's father probably did not notice. After all, he was still only eleven years old.

The nun told him to go inside and play with his old friends while she spent some time with his aunt.

After a couple of hours, the nun returned and he asked her when he was going home.

YOU ARE HOME...she told him.

That kind of betrayal would drive anyone to drink, EB thought to himself when he reflected on his father's dreadful and possibly disastrous early years. But EB always believed that his dad's drinking problem was a physical thing. His father simply couldn't handle alcohol. It was in the genes. He loved to hang around the corner saloon with the big drinkers, but he was a small drinker. After ten drinks, the big guys were still standing tall at the bar. After three drinks, EB's father was stooped and swaying out the door.

Or should have been.

Certainly this sad situation was not unusual in EB's neighborhood. His Uncle Rob, who lived upstairs, was a problem drinker, too. To EB and his friends, the image of the drunken Irish father was no mere cliché. It was everyday life.

But that meant that almost everyday, life was a nightmare for the wives and kids.

EB's mother was a pretty, slim, petite woman with beautiful pale blue eyes. And, it was said, the most beautiful legs in Brooklyn. She was usually very quiet. Undemonstrative. Stoic. She was a strict, physical disciplinarian with EB and Dorothy when she had to be, but otherwise she received the blows of her everyday life with an accepting silence.

That, too, was not unusual in EB's neighborhood.

She had a quick, musical laugh. Very high-pitched and light. Like the sound of crystal wind chimes. Her big passion was her "programs". Every afternoon it was a must that she listen to "Stella Dallas" and "Mary Noble, Backstage Wife" on the radio. There were a few years when EB and Dorothy were growing up that she had to go to work because their father was in and out of a Veterans Hospital somewhere up in the Bronx, drying out perhaps, the kids never knew. And later in her life, she actually had a steady job for a short period of time. Then, it must have disappointed her greatly to miss her "programs".

But she never complained.

And she did not drink. EB never saw his mother drink more than one glass of wine in any social situation. More often, it was a glass or two of ginger ale. EB figured that because her husband always had too much, she always had too little.

But she was an expert on the drinking man.

Sometimes on paydays, early, right after 6PM, she would send EB, even at the tender age of seven or eight, around the corner to McDade's Saloon to tell his father it was time to come home.

Later than 6:30PM would be too late. Then his father wouldn't listen.

SUPPOSIN' HE'S NOT THERE?...EB would ask...HE'S THERE...she would say...AND DON'T COME BACK WITHOUT HIM.

EB did it, but he didn't like it.

And his father liked it a lot less.

But most of the time it worked because it embarrassed his father to see his little son edge his way into that smelly saloon, hesitant, tentative, a little frightened, but determined to stick it out. And it didn't hurt any that the other men urged him to go home with his son.

After a prolonged binge, or after a particularly horrible night, EB's mother would ask him to have a "talk" with his father. She'd awaken him early, at 5AM, and leave the two of them alone in the kitchen. A seven or eight year old kid begging, pleading, lecturing, and hectoring his hung-over father about the dangers of demon rum.

Heartbreaking.

Those were the moments when EB himself felt like crying (but did not, of course). All too frequently it was a tough life, and inside the sanctity of his head, he railed at the gods for that. But on the other hand, it sure made a kid grow up in a big hurry.

And sometimes being a Christian offered helpful insights.

At St. Vincent Ferrer (EB's grammar school), the nuns taught the kids that because Adam and Eve sinned, they were expelled from Paradise. And because they sinned, we were all born with the stain of original sin on our souls. In essence, we were all paying for that original sin. So Paradise on earth was out of the question.

Therefore, in terms of your own life...hey, what could you expect, right?

EB's sister Dorothy was two years younger. They were close. He appreciated her warmth, her loyalty, and (as he fancied it) her little sister adoration. He was fond of adoration.

He always thought she was a very beautiful girl. And she was. They were friends as well as brother and sister.

Always.

No matter what.

They talked to each other a lot, about everything. But particularly about their family "troubles". There were no secrets between them; they held nothing back. Their points of view were expressed freely and honestly. As they grew older, they would sit together in the living room after their parents had gone to sleep and share observations and opinions about everything that touched their lives. They supported each other. They were there for each other.

Always.

But one frightening day, early on, EB almost wasn't there for his sister, or for anyone else. Because on one freezing winter afternoon he almost got himself killed.

Precisely because he was a wiseguy.

It was one of those "Ice Days" in Brooklyn, New York. One of those extreme examples of global cooling. Everything was ice. Trees, lawns, roofs, stoops, sidewalks were covered with a thick coat of translucent frozen sleet that a temperature in the low teens kept from melting. The ice covered the bulk of an earlier snow storm and held the lumps, humps, and drifted shapes on the houses, lawns, and sidewalks and in the street in a kind of weirdly beautiful suspended animation. The relatively infrequent passing cars had formed two deep, eight or nine-inch troughs down the center of the street, like the storied wagon ruts on the Oregon Trail...only wider. And the semi-shiny slippery ice preserved the shapes of the troughs.

The air was arctic. There was no wind.

The cold didn't need any help.

People were indoors. Nothing stirred. Nothing moved.

Except EB. He was out because no one else was. When everyone zigged, EB tended to zag. He was a wiseguy, and wiseguys were always interested in the possibilities of the unusual and the unexpected.

The very moment it dawned, this day established itself as unusual.

And the unexpected was on its way.

EB was six years old and stood in the rear of the driveway between his neighbor's house and his own. It was no wider than six feet. Not nearly wide enough for a car. In Brooklyn, you called it a driveway even though you could not drive your way through it.

He was dressed in a heavy tan cloth mackinaw with a faux sheepskin shawl collar. It was high-thigh length, and he wore it over green corduroy knickers. The coat always made him feel like a cowboy. He loved it. (And was very pleased when, fifteen years later, Jim Arness stole the look and used it on "Gunsmoke".) On his head was a knitted tan and brown woolen cap pulled down over his ears, and his feet, up to mid-shin, were covered with black rubber galoshes that slipped over his shoes and socks and closed with three metal buckles.

He faced down the driveway, which slanted away from him at a very cooperative downward angle toward the street, and he smiled with anticipation as the slick ice-covered surface sparkled dimly, dirtily, evilly back at him. In his mittened hands he was holding a family sled "borrowed" from his cellar. He assumed it was his cousin Bob's sled, but he didn't bother asking.

Wiseguys didn't ask. Wiseguys took what they were given, or what they could get. No big plan. No long-range strategy. Wiseguys were action oriented. Wiseguys reacted to the moment, the immediate situation.

And this moment, right there before him, EB was given a gift from the gods, an icy, slick, launching pad that he knew would make a sled go like hell. And going like hell was exactly what he intended to do.

He took three running steps, bellywhopped onto the sled and zoomed down the driveway.

Did he scout out the route beforehand, checking for bare spots, obstacles, or unexpected movement on the sidewalk?

Never thought of it.

Did he worry about, or even know about, the blind spot created by the car parked to his right in front of his neighbor's house?

Of course not.

Did he wish he had a lookout at the end of the driveway to warn him of any oncoming traffic?

Awww, there wouldn't be any traffic.

At the building line, the driveway angled more steeply to the street and EB picked up speed. He shot across the sidewalk and flew off the curb and into the middle of East 40th Street.

And was hit by a car.

Of course later it would be called a miracle that he wasn't killed. His mother swore it. His grandmother professed it. And EB believed it.

But there was a more rational explanation.

When it appeared that EB was about to go under the front tires, he was on the high point, or the saddle, of the two troughs, so he was on a higher level, almost nine inches higher, than the tires and closer to the height of the front bumper. The moment he saw the approaching car to his right, he instinctively rolled to his left, carrying the sled with him, using it as a shield. The driver no doubt stood on his brakes and thus locked the wheels. As the car slid along the icy troughs and into EB, the bumper hooked the sled runner and simply pushed the sled and EB behind it for about forty yards down the center of the slippery street until it finally stopped.

The panicked driver leapt from the car, slipped on the ice, went down, got up, slipped again and, regaining his feet, rushed to the front of his car terrified of what he would find.

He found a startled, shaken little kid staring up at him. Obviously EB was scared out of his mind, but not his wits. Even at the age of six he had a feel for the code (you did not cry). Lying there with a sled half covering his body, the kid did not say a word, but the look on his face said...WHAT THE HELL ARE YOU DOING ON MY BLOCK?...

The driver could not immediately tell if the kid was hurt, but the look of surprise had slowly changed to an intriguing, almost intimidating, Mona Lisa-like smile, so he didn't seem to be.

The sled appeared to be undamaged. That was a good sign...and the man dared to take this first breath.

Maybe the ice had saved them both.

The driver asked EB if anything hurt; he shook his head no. The driver asked EB if he could talk; he nodded his head yes and, in response to the next question, gave the stranger his address. The man cradled EB in his arms, carried him back to his house (that's what you did in the '40s), and rang the bell. EB's mom answered and understandably reacted hysterically to what she saw. She cried, screamed, prayed, and questioned as she directed the man to carry EB into the kitchen and lay the well-bundled body on the table. By now EB's grandmother was down from her upstairs apartment and, in turn, his mother and grand-mother touched, felt, prodded, unhooked, unbuttoned, and care-fully examined him while EB protested and proclaimed his well-being and the poor man, the poor panic stricken stranger, did the only dying in the room.

Finally, while they thanked God, the good Lord, the Blessed Mother, the communion of saints, and swore that EB's guardian angel was really looking over him this day, the ladies pronounced him unhurt and allowed the grateful stranger to return to his car.

A guardian angel looking out for him! His mother had said it. Later, EB mulled that one over. He was fascinated by the possibilities of it. An angel of his own protecting him, keeping him safe. What a concept! An angel to watch over him...just him. It was like he was bullet proof. His mother said it. And mothers knew everything! Mothers were never wrong. So he never forgot those words. Those wonderful, mystical words.

Words to live by.

And he did.

That sense of invincibility stayed with him for the rest of his life. It instilled a sense of physical daring. And it added an insouciance, a light-hearted zest to his life, and a step to his saunter.

The twinkle.

Chapter Two-The Family And The Neighborhood **2**

Bob Campbell was the perpetrator. The one who gave EB his oddball nickname.

It was late spring 1939, EB was around four years old, almost five, and had a green tricycle that he raced all around the vicinity of 791 East 40th Street. Up and down everybody's driveway, back and forth on the sidewalks in front of everyone's house. Up and down, back and forth.

Incessantly.

Chatting, prattling to everyone he saw. He talked to everybody, and when no one was around, he talked to himself, and when he tired of that, he talked to his tricycle.

Incessantly.

At this time, his cousin Bob came into possession of a green derby hat with the legend "Erin Go Braugh" emblazoned across the front. It was undoubtedly left over from St. Patrick's Day. The derby was not what you would call top of the line. It was made of cardboard. But the significant factor in the design was that the "E" of Erin and the "B" of Braugh were emphasized. So when you looked at the front of the hat, the first thing you noticed was a giant E and an equally sized giant B.

Bob gave that derby hat to his little cousin. He even made up a little jingle to go with it.

The lyrics are lost to antiquity.

Something about a green tricycle, a green derby, and a green EB. The jingle ended with a line close to "...he's wearin' the green...the bike is green, the derby is green, even EB is green".

EB loved that derby; he wore it everyday, everywhere. And always sung his own version of Bob's jingle. Especially when he was riding his green tricycle. Pretty soon, the whole block was referring to him as..."EB and his derby". And then the derby frizzled and crumbled, as cardboard will, and disappeared. But the "EB" appellation endured.

Cardboard hats don't last long.

But nicknames last forever.

Especially in a small town like Brooklyn, New York.

Today, Brooklyn is a city of over two and a half million people. The population was almost the same during the '40s and '50s. But Brooklyn was a different place.

In EB's time, Brooklyn was the biggest small town in the country. Maybe the world. There was a constancy, a consistency, a dependable texture to everyday life. People stayed put; nobody moved. Consequently, everybody knew everybody. And watched out for everybody. And, in their own unobtrusive way, cared about everybody. They didn't talk about that necessarily.

They just lived it.

The neighborhood grocery store owner, the candy store, drug store and delicatessen owners knew EB from the day he was born. They watched him grow up. They watched all the kids grow up. They saw it all. Smiled at most of it. Shook their heads at some of it.

Constancy.

Brooklyn then was a collection of neighborhoods. Ethnic entities. Everybody had his own space. Very politically incorrect by today's standards. Irish, Italian, German, Negro, Catholic, Jewish, and other nationalities had their own areas with distinct

14

borders. Protestants were the exception. Only Protestants didn't have their own space.

They had everybody's space. They were everywhere.

Ubiquitous. Indigenous.

You knew where each other's turf began and ended. And while you were within someone else's borders, you were a guest. You respected the prevailing mores, customs, beliefs. You showed no disrespect, you did no posturing, no politicking; you acted like a guest because you knew it was the thing to do. It was not written down anywhere, it wasn't the law, it wasn't talked about, you just knew it. And you just did it. And because of that mutual respect, you could go anywhere, at any time. Three o'clock in the morning was as safe as three o'clock in the afternoon. Of course there were exceptions to that, but basically the whole thing worked. It was former Mayor David Dinkins' "Gorgeous Mosaic" before we defined it, organized it, and legislated it to death.

EB's Brooklyn was very Catholic. Especially his neighborhood of East Flatbush. In those days, when you met kids you didn't know, you didn't ask what neighborhood they came from; you asked what parish they belonged to. (Of course, if you made the serious faux pas of asking that of a Protestant, you got the famous arched eyebrow look..."You friggin' immigrant".)

EB's parish was St. Vincent Ferrer. On Glenwood Road. Its three-story orange brick building took up the whole block from 38th to 37th Street. The church itself was on the ground floor. Cavernous and rather austere, it sat seven hundred true believers. (And maybe a few believers who were faking it a little.) The upper two floors were the grammar school, 1A through 8B. The school was under the tight control of the dreaded Dominican nuns. They were committed teachers and relentless disciplinarians. Unlike some of his friends, EB had a great, albeit secret, admiration for the nuns.

Even though they beat the crap out of him.

Or maybe because they beat the crap out of him.

The nuns were smart, dedicated, and businesslike. Very tough. They had to be. They had about 45 kids in every class, and they had to control the few wackos of the class or lose control of the whole class. So they whacked the wackos.

EB respected that.

St. Vincent Ferrer was the center of EB's neighborhood. Not only religiously and culturally, but geographically. Glenwood Road,the street the church fronted, ran approximately east-west. Paralleling it on the north were Farragut Road and Foster Avenue. South of Glenwood Road were the alphabet avenues...H, I and J.

Completing the grid were the north-south numbered streets. 37th Street to 31st and Flatbush Avenue west of the church and 38th Street to 49th and Utica Avenue to the east.

The houses were mostly single family detached and semi-detached on 30' by 50' lots. Lots of brick below and wooden siding above. Some of the detached houses were white clapboard colonials with wooden porches across the front. All well kept, of course, with small front lawns and equally small and mostly fenced backyards. Some homes had one-car garages in the backyard linked to the street by usable car-width driveways.

And stoops. Everyone had a well-used stoop. Even two. The houses were built so high above the level of the street and back so far that double stoops were necessary. You walked up a few steps to a level area then climbed more steps to the front door. It was as if the streets were laid out in the bottom of gullies and the houses were built on the banks.

There were two other distinguishing characteristics of EB's neighborhood.

The first was trees! Beautiful old trees. Almost every house had one in front between the curb and the sidewalk. There were maples, sycamores, pin oaks, white oaks, and many linden and elm trees (before the Dutch Elm disease decimated them). On some blocks, the overarching trees formed a continuous canopy. (You couldn't even play stickball on 39th Street because of that impenetrable cover. A serious problem.)

The second was the most mysterious, the most unexpected. They called it the "woods"....a one-square mile anomaly of primal Brooklyn forest. It couldn't have existed; it shouldn't have existed.

But it did.

EB thought of it as his own Sherwood Forest.

16

If only he had a horse, he thought. (Riding a horse through the "woods" was his favorite fantasy.)

In length, the woods started at Albany Avenue (41st Street) and rambled and gamboled down to Nostrand Avenue (30th). In width, it extended from Farragut Road to Foster Avenue, which was then a dirt road. The woods had thick stands of old trees...oaks, maples, chestnuts, sycamores...and large open areas of erosion-rutted bare hills. It had a small, running stream from which the little kids took sips of fresh, cool water. It had glens, and meadows. It had hard-packed dirt trails and, down by Nostrand Avenue, sandy soil and weeping willow trees. It was dark and it was light. It had knobby hills and grassy hummocks.

To EB, it was magical. And beautiful.

And bountiful in the sense that it provided the kids of EB's neighborhood with everything they needed. In winter, they used its slopes and hills to sleigh ride. Hundreds of kids going up and down, up and down the different trails on different hills. Orderly, organized, smooth. And not a parent to be seen.

In summer, they took refuge in its cool, dark and hidden places. And they played baseball on a kid-designed, rut-ridden field called the "plateau". Later, when they were older, and better, they played more organized ball on the big field, called "Kings Field", down near Nostrand Avenue. The semi-pro Corsairs played there on Sunday afternoons.

And EB played there on Saturday mornings.

Amazing.

Magical.

That was the parish.

It was surrounded by other parishes, other schools, other neighborhoods.

But that was EB's parish and EB's neighborhood.

And it was fine.

East of 41st Street (which was known as Albany Avenue) was the end of the world.

There were blocks of underdeveloped land, open lots, low factory buildings, an abandoned brewery and occasional houses on unpaved streets. Such a street was East 42nd Street. On that street on a Saturday morning in the spring of 1942, EB was following a trio of older (by four or five years) and much bigger boys. They were his cousin John, their neighbor Gilly Hefner, and the legendary Harold "Skippy" Devoy.

EB's classmate Benny Desmond lived on the end of that street in an old, ramshackle, brown house. It was the only house on the block and there was always a number of chickens pecking around in front of it. What they could possible find there to eat was a mystery to EB. The entire street was dirt. Black dirt. EB always thought the street was made of coal. The surface of that street was all opposing angles...up and down, back and forth. Deep ruts and rain gullies pockmarked the surface from beginning to end. This was not a street to drive a car on.

But EB and the older boys didn't care about that; they were walking. Not to Benny Desmond's house, but to a low, two-story factory building in the middle of the block. John wanted to climb to the roof of that factory. Why did John want to climb that building? He didn't say.

And nobody asked. Nobody questioned it. That's what they were there for, and that's what they would do. And it was not that difficult, even for EB, who was almost eight years old at this time. There were some barrels, contents a mystery, piled two tiers high next to the south wall of the building. They used those to reach the first crook of a large, very high tree that overhung the top of the factory building. Because EB was so small, they had to reach down and swing him up into the tree, but once in the tree, EB was in his element. (Tarzan yell here.) He easily followed the other boys as they climbed high into the tree, shimmied out onto a thick overhanging branch, and, using a smaller branch, swung down onto the black tarred flat roof.

It was about ten o'clock in the morning, and there they were on the roof. Now what? It was a pretty nice day, the sun was out, but the view was hardly spectacular. This was, after all, 42nd Street.

Directly below them looking to the west were the roofs of the garages belonging to the houses on Albany Avenue. They were looking at the rear of those houses about thirty feet away and about even with the second floors.

The bedroom floors.

Other than that, and that wasn't much, the view was a non event. Then one of the boys observed that there was somebody looking at them from one of the bedroom windows. They all took a casual look as the window opened and a kid about John's age (twelve) started yelling at them to get off the roof. They gave him the finger in unison.

He smiled enigmatically, like an earlier incarnation of Clint Eastwood, brought up his BB gun and commenced firing.

The keeper of the roof! (Self appointed, of course.) Just doing his job as he saw it. The sheriff...blazing away at the bad guys with his Red Ryder.

PING, PING, PING...EB and the boys went prone. There was a lip of about a foot around the perimeter of the roof, topped with ceramic tiles.

Not deep enough to hide them. And the kid was slightly above them.

Advantage his.

To make matters worse this kid was not a bad shot. He was using the ceramic tiles to ricochet the BBs into the boys. BBs didn't kill you but they stung you. They were all yelling to each other and, to be brutally frank, about to panic. At that point, John gave the order to abandon the roof. Over the side, he said, onto the garage roof directly below.

That roof was peaked and would get them out of the line of fire. As a group they rose, and one by one they jumped from the factory roof to the garage roof eight feet below.

All except EB. He wasn't gonna bail out like a chickenshit. This guy wasn't the law; he was just a kid. EB started screaming at the kid in the window. All the time giving him a double salute...The left palm jammed into the crook of the right arm with the right hand extended straight up and (to make it a really disrespectful) with the middle finger of the right hand stabbing at the sky.

BA FONGUL! BA FONGUL!...(the only Italian he knew, or thought he knew), EB screamed.

John yelled up at him...GET DOWN HERE, YOU LITTLE JERK...JUMP...JUMP...JUMP...YOU'RE GONNA GET HURT...HE'S GONNA PLUG YOU...JUMP...I'LL CATCH YOU...John stood with his arms outstretched and screamed at EB.

The Red Ryder screamed back in its own unique way.

The first BB skimmed off the tiles and hit EB just above the knee. The second hit higher up on the thigh. That lesson learned, EB moved smartly to the roof edge, took one quick look at the garage roof below where the other two boys lay prone and John waited with open arms, and leapt out into space.

He didn't see the telephone cable until it caught him under the neck.

He hung there by his neck for what seemed to him to be ten minutes, at least.

But of course it was only a fraction of a second before he reached up and grabbed the cable with two hands and took a life sustaining breath. He was afraid to just hang there, afraid of the shooter. So he got a little swing going and dropped into the waiting arms of his cousin and his friends.

They all lay behind the peak of the garage roof, now hidden from the wacko kid in the window...and giggled. They made noises about killing that little son of a bitch and stealing the Red Ryder (which they all coveted), but of course they would do no such thing. They would not seek revenge.

It was a violation of the code.

The kid beat them fair and square. It was his turf.

They waited until the kid in the window lost interest. Then all together jumped from the garage roof onto the backyard grass, rolled once (very important, very aesthetic), leapt gracefully to their feet and exited, chattering happily, onto Albany Avenue.

And walked back to East 40th Street.

On the way, EB thought about what had just happened. He figured John knew about the crazy kidshooter. Heard about it, probably, and wanted to check it out himself. John surely never figured that anybody would or could get hurt.

EB was OK with that. He'd never say anything to John. He had a scary, thrilling, and confidence-building experience. He was happy John asked him to come along.

EB was only eight.

And already he was one of them.

Chapter Three-The Maturing Wiseguy 3

By the end of 1947, EB was growing comfortable in the skin of a wiseguy. He was maturing. Playing his little games, laughing, teasing, testing, busting chops when it suited him.

Christmas evening of that year, he and Dorothy left the house together. She was eleven years old, EB was thirteen. It was around 8PM on one of those sparkling clear winter nights. They talked about the brightness of the moon and stars as they walked on East 40th Street toward Glenwood Road where they would take a left and head to the neighborhood candy store. Pease's candy store. Mr. Malcolm Pease, proprietor.

Everybody knew Mr. Pease and Mr. Pease knew everybody.

It was Christmas, so the store was kind of deserted, just two small groups of teenagers were hanging around at the back tables. Mr. Pease had a pot bellied stove back there, so it was a pleasant place to be on a winter's night.

Mr. Pease himself was at home with his family, so there was another teenager working the store.

EB and Dorothy had a dollar each, slipped to them by their Uncle Rob that afternoon. It was his usual Christmas gift. It wasn't much, but it was appreciated.

Naturally, they couldn't wait to spend it.

EB and his sister sat at the front counter and had egg creams. Then picked out a couple boxes of their favorite candies (Juicy Fruits and Good 'n Plenty for EB), paid their bills and headed home. As they rounded the corner of 40th Street, EB again turned his attention to the clear and bright winter sky. But this time he noticed something he had not seen before.

The moon was full or almost full. Nothing unusual about that, but surrounding the moon at about two-moon widths was a defined circular haze.

A golden rim.

EB told Dorothy to look and concentrate on that rim. He told her it was a rare phenomenon. Happened only once or twice a century. It foretold a great storm descending upon the land. Tomorrow, the wiseguy told his little sister, there will be a blizzard.

Of course he was wingin' it. Just havin' a little fun. And she would have known it, too, if she could have seen his eyes. She knew the twinkle.

But it was too dark to see it that night.

Now all he had to worry about was how he would weasel out of this the next morning.

As it turned out, he had nothing to worry about.

The date was December 26, 1947.

That day Brooklyn received the largest snowfall in its history...24 inches.

Whew! Wow!

What luck.

Or...could it be? Is it possible? Do guardian angels have a sense of humor?

Naah, couldn't be.

Could it?

And a few weeks later...

This was a Saturday in middle January, 1948. Maybe two o'clock in the afternoon. It was cold, but not too bad. A hazy winter sun tried but barely moved the temperature over forty degrees. Here and there on the lawns of the mostly single family semi-detached homes of EB's Flatbush neighborhood there were piles of dirty snow from the ten-inch snowfall of the previous week. The street and sidewalks were clean and mostly dry, but the snow clung in yellowish clumps to the now dormant grassy areas next to the curb and on the lawns and around and under bushes. It was one of those forgettable days between New Year's Day and April 15th when nothing happens. This day was just a number on a calendar. It was mandated to happen, it had to take place, but nobody would ever remember this day.

Except EB.

He had turned onto East 40th Street from Glenwood Road. He was thirteen years old. And bored. Resigned to the anonymity of the day. Feeling pretty anonymous himself. And that was not a good feeling for EB.

About three quarters of the way down the block he saw his cousin John coming toward him. Probably coming from the house they shared. John was, in all honesty, a pretty strange dude himself, which was why EB considered him a living legend.

Hero worship.

On this day, as always, John was accompanied by his friend Harold "Skippy" Devoy, the demi-god. There was no one else on the block. EB immediately saw some possiblilities in this situation. When he was certain they saw him, he gave his favorite sign of greeting.

The arm.

The old Italian ba fongul!

EB knew it would be enough. And it was.

John and Skippy took off and began to close the hundred yards between them in a hurry. Malevolence in their bearing, mayhem in their teenage hearts.

With a shout of glee, EB ducked into the driveway on his right. The hunt was on, the dogs were loosed, but the fox was the fastest kid on East 40th Street. And he knew the backyards of his block better than anyone. When he reached the yard, he turned left, in the direction from which John and Skippy were coming.

He could see almost halfway down the block, a series of tiny (maybe 30' by 20') grassy plots. Most, but not all, were bordered by three to five foot high fences of varying construction and design. They were statements of ownership, "this is mine", not designed to keep anyone out. Or in. Unless there was a dog. But on this side of the street at that time, there were no dogs. That was good. EB had no use for dogs.

He took a running dive over the first fence, rolled, and up and running, jumped the next. He used a very familiar tree limb to swing over the next (the Tarzan yell here), sprinted through a few yards with no fences between them, and, with the grace of an Olympian, hurdled the next three footer. There was a snow pile spanning the next fence; he went full out in the air and tobogganed over it. At full speed, he approached the next fence, a five-footer made with two-by-fours and chicken wire. He put his right hand on the flat top and vaulted over it as pretty as you please. He was now at the Bohan house, just a few houses this side of his own. And a hundred yards or so down the block from where he started.

He casually walked down the alley and stood on the sidewalk, and waited. John and Skippy appeared on the sidewalk just a few houses this side of where EB had disappeared. Still those hundred yards away from their quarry.

And now genuinely pissed off.

Instinctively understanding that, and laughing, EB flipped them the bird.

And here they came again.

EB pivoted and at full speed disappeared into the Bohan driveway. But as soon as he reached the building line, he stopped. He knew that trick wasn't going to work again. He hoped he was still one step ahead of these two guys but was under no illusions. It was only a matter of time until he was caught, if he played the game honorably and did not cheat by going off East 40th Street.

And EB did not cheat. He knew the code.

The Bohan house had a high red brick front stoop; EB used it to hide himself as he took a peek. John and Skippy were not in sight. As EB had hoped they would, they had ducked into different driveways to try to trap him in a classic pincer move.

EB simply walked across the street.

And, in plain sight, walked back up the street toward Glenwood Road where he had started this little war game. Carefully watching the other side of the street as he went.

John and Skip appeared across the street, about halfway down the block.

And started walking toward him. Walking.

Oh, oh.

The game was getting serious.

EB ducked into the nearest driveway, reached the backyard, and pondered his problem. Toward Glenwood Road. there were only a few houses left. Not much room to maneuver. Not much choice. He went the other way. Got a few houses down and saw Skippy coming at him, maybe four houses away. Coming fast and having no problem with fences. Damn those demi-gods! EB turned and began moving in the opposite direction. He figured John was waiting for him in one of the driveways back there. It was a crapshoot. If EB picked the right one, he was gone again; if he picked the wrong one, he was gone all right.

EB hopped two fences and turned into that driveway.

Right into the arms of cousin John.

They took him over to 39th Street. On the other side of Glenwood Road, there was a house on the corner with a big lawn that swept down on about a forty-five degree angle. They laid EB out on the lawn. They had removed his jacket, his shirt, and his undershirt.

And piled snow on his bare chest.

There were no restraints.

There was only the code.

Honor.

But just in case, they had his clothes. And told him he'd get them back if he did not move for five minutes. And they'd be watching.

The problem was it was getting very close to four o'clock and the temperature was moving in the wrong direction.

EB was screaming about mercy and cruelty, bloodlines and the gene pool, when an elderly (about 45) woman appeared on the corner. She approached warily. EB explained the situation as calmly has he could...TWO HIGH SCHOOL KIDS HE DIDN'T KNOW HAD TO DO THIS EXPERIMENT FOR BIOLOGY

CLASS...AND THEY PICKED ON HIM BECAUSE HE WAS SMALL...AND THEY HAD HIS CLOTHES WITH THEM WHERE THEY WERE HIDING IN THE BUSHES THERE ACROSS THE STREET...AND THEY KNEW WHERE HE LIVED...AND THEY SAID IF HE MOVED THEY WOULD GO TO HIS HOUSE AND BEAT UP HIS LITTLE SISTER...AND HE WAS GETTING SO COLD HE MIGHT BE READY TO PASS OUT...The elderly lady turned around and yelled at the bushes across the street, demanding those clothes.

No response.

Mmmmm.

Then EB told the woman that...HE WAS TOO COLD TO MOVE, AND ANYWAY IT WOULDN'T DO ANY GOOD...HE HAD TO PROTECT HIS SISTER'S LIFE...BUT PERHAPS IF SHE WENT ACROSS THE STREET AND WENT AFTER THEM, THOSE BULLIES WOULD GIVE UP...AND OH BY THE WAY, HE DIDN'T KNOW THEIR NAMES BUT HE KNEW WHAT HIGH SCHOOL THEY WENT TO...IT WAS MIDWOOD...AND MAYBE IF SHE MENTIONED THAT, IT MIGHT HELP.

She did all of that. And before she got halfway across the street, EB' s clothes flew out of the bushes.

He knew they were gone then. He got up, brushed off the snow, thanked that kindly old lady, retrieved his clothes, and got dressed.

That was close. He didn't give them up, didn't squeal, didn't break the code. OK, he did bend it a little, but that was just taking advantage of the situation. Strategy.

EB was a wiseguy.

But he was no dummy.

4

EB had another cousin.

His name was Matty.

Matthew, son of Uncle Matt and Aunt Florence (EB's mother's sister). Brother of Anne, Barbara, and Paul. They lived in a semi-detached house on East 39th Street between Glenwood Road and Avenue "H", just around the corner from EB's house.

EB had a lot of cousins. He thought of them as his immediate family. He thought of them as brothers and sisters. He considered Uncle Matt and Aunt Flo to be his surrogate parents.

And there were times when he needed them to be just that.

And they always were.

They were very good to EB and his sister. They made sure that every Christmas there was a respectable number of gifts under the tree. Gifts that EB's mother and father could not afford. In fact, for years whatever Matty found under his Christmas tree,

EB found under his. And Aunt Flo and Uncle Matt did the same for Dorothy. They treated EB and Dorothy as if they were their own kids.

EB and Dorothy cherished their love and many kindnesses.

Appreciated them. Valued them.

And never forgot.

EB and Matty were almost the same age. Only six months separated them. They were practically twins. Good pals, constant companions, and intense competitors. They did everything together, and each tried to do everything better than the other. Everything was a game, a contest. The competition was always there, but never overt, never stated, except in fun. And that was the key; it was a friendly rivalry...you won quietly, modestly...and you lost with a smile. They both understood that their sparring better prepared them for the bigger events.

Matty was blue-eyed and blonde. EB had brown hair and hazel eyes (his father's eyes). They were both about the same size...not tall when they were young and destined never to be...but they had good bodies. Strong and broad-shouldered. Their daily competition sharpened them, and made them both better. Consequently, when it came to sports or other things physical, they did everything well. If truth be told, Matty probably had a slight edge in most things, basketball for sure. But EB had something Matty did not, and that was speed, which made up for a lot.

Athletes, both.

From age six to age twelve, EB spent more time on Matty's block than he did on his own. Because that's where Matty was.

And that's where Harold Brice was.

Harold was another close friend. The third member of this triumvirate...this sometime unwholesome threesome...this unholy trinity. These three stayed together from the time they entered grammar school until the time they graduated. Growing up they were tight. From ages six to fourteen they were close. Once they entered high school, the relationship loosened a bit until age eighteen, when they drifted apart.

They learned about life with each other and from each

other.

Harold was not the athlete that EB and Matty were. He did not have the body or the daring. Physically he was timid, hesitant, frozen, unwilling to expose his body to potential risk. At seven or eight years years of age, when EB and Matty climbed one of the neighborhood trees, it took them just a few seconds to reach the higher reaches where the branches were thin and swaying; while Harold remained on the larger and sturdier branches on the lower part of the tree. At eleven and twelve, when EB and Matty visited their "clubhouse" on Mulligan's garage roof, Harold was the last up, and when they leapt off into Mulligan's backyard, which they did routinely, they had to stop and take the time to coax Harold to follow them. And he never did master the technique (the art) of leaping, hitting the grass, rolling once, and in one motion, coming up on the toes ready to go. It was a Gene Kelly move and not for the ballet-impaired.

And in their early teens, when EB and Matty swung from garage roof to garage roof on telephone cables, Harold always got tired in the middle and dropped off. So Harold was not quite the strong, bold, fearless jock that his two friends fancied themselves to be. But that was not held against him.

No. Harold had other talents that were missing in EB and Matty.

Harold was socially adept.

Harold was comfortable in polite society.

Harold was smooth.

Harold was good with the girls.

Harold always had money.

And Harold was generous with everything he had .

By the time they were eleven years old, the three of them were beyond the stage of just experimenting with cigarettes. By then they were smokers, not completely hooked yet, but close. Harold always seemed to have money for a carton of Old Golds, which he hid in his garage. And that was one place where the three of them smoked their butts. At home, EB occasionally pilfered one of his father's Pall Malls and smoked it in the cellar.

One morning in the late spring of 1945, when they were around the age of eleven, Harold gave EB and Matty ten dollars apiece. Just gave it to them. A grand gift! No, a bonanza! They should have questioned him, but they didn't. Of course they wondered about this windfall, thought it smelled of sin, but they didn't ask Harold any questions, probably because they were afraid of the answers.

That afternoon, the three of them took their thirty dollars down to Utica Avenue, where nobody knew them, and bought three cartons of cigarettes and a bagful of junk food. They spent the rest of the afternoon in a vast empty lot on the east side of Utica Avenue that was like an equatorial jungle to the three boys. The lot was a block long and half a block wide. It was overgrown with small weed-like trees and choked with poison sumac, poison ivy, and a hundred variations of high and low growing weeds the boys could not identify by name. It had a small stream running through it with a resident frog population, a million mosquitoes and a multitude of dragonflies. It was another neighborhood anomaly, another surprising, exotic, foreign environment allowed to exist in the Brooklyn of the '40s and '50s. It was as if someone had taken a tiny piece of the Amazon jungle and plunked it down in Brooklyn. And everybody said, "Oh, OK..." and didn't seem to notice the implausibility of it.

EB, Matty, and Harold thought of the lot as their private jungle retreat and that afternoon they stayed there for a few hours smoking and eating candy, Cracker Jacks, and pretzels. They were rich.

EB went home that evening and hid his cigarettes along with the remainder of his ten dollars in the bottom of the bedroom closet he shared with his father. He stuffed the carton under a pile of sweaters. His father would never notice, he was sure.

A few nights later, EB was lying on the living room floor listening to the Lone Ranger on the radio. He hardly noticed when the front door bell rang. His dad, home early and sober, went out into the vestibule to greet the caller. Still EB did not notice. But after some minutes, he became aware of muffled voices in serious-sounding conversation. And suddenly, his street-kid antennae were tingling.

Oh, oh.

A moment later, his dad, Harold, and Harold's very upset father entered EB's living room and stood there looking over at EB lying on the floor. EB's father motioned for him to join them in the dining room and he did so reluctantly.

This was trouble.

Mr. Brice looked at EB and said...DID HAROLD GIVE YOU TEN DOLLARS?...EB looked at Harold and saw the dreaded look of defeat there. Snagged, he thought to himself. It never occurred to EB to lie. It was not his, or their way. When you were nailed, you were nailed, that's it. No weaseling. No lying. Stand up and take it like Captain America. That was the code.

YES, HE DID...said EB, head down...DID YOU KNOW THAT HE STOLE IT FROM HIS GRANDMOTHER?...NO...answered EB, head lower...WHERE DID YOU THINK HE GOT IT FROM?...challenged Mr. Brice...I DIDN'T KNOW...whispered EB...WHY DIDN'T YOU KNOW?...pressed Mr. Brice...I DIDN'T ASK HIM...mumbled EB, his head on his chest now, staring at the floor looking for a hole...SPEAK NO EVIL, HEAR NO EVIL, SEE NO EVIL...Mr. Brice said to EB's father...DID YOU SPEND IT ALL?...asked EB's father...NO...said EB...WHERE IS IT?...GO GET WHATEVER YOU HAVE...NOW!...commanded his father. EB disappeared and returned with a carton of Pall Malls with six dollars and change filling the space of one missing pack of cigarettes. Still looking at the floor, he handed it to his father. Who in turn handed it to Mr. Brice.

EB's father offered to reimburse Mr. Brice for the missing money but Mr. Brice said that was not necessary. He shook hands with EB's father, patted EB on the head, took Harold by the arm and turned to leave.

Through the whole thing, Harold never said a word. But EB didn't blame him for that. There wasn't a whole lot to say. Who knew what he went through at home. And if either one of them had tried to bullshit his way through this he would have been caught in a lie and whacked around the room by his father, although that was still a distinct possibility for EB.

EB's father showed Mr. Brice and Harold out the front door and came back into the dining room. He moved toward EB with a menacing look and EB backed away a few steps.

His father kept coming.

And EB kept going.

Pretty soon, his father was chasing EB around the dining room table.

EB tried to stay a full diameter away around the oval table. And could have kept it up for the rest of the night.

But why?

Sooner or later he was going to get it. So it might as well be sooner. And his father, who was not that young, was getting tired, and that strenuous activity could have been dangerous to him...so EB stopped.

Ready to take his medicine.

His father took off his belt and whomped him across the buttocks a half dozen times. It hurt a little, not too bad. But to EB the real pain was emotional. That was the first time that his father had ever taken off his belt to him. He'd heard other kids talk about a whomping with their fathers' belts, but this was a first for him. And he thought to himself that his father must have been really disappointed in his son that night.

And that hurt big-time...not in the buttocks, but in the heart.

Later that evening in a softer moment, his father explained that he could not abide stealing. For him, stealing was the most heinous crime because it was a gross violation of the other person's dignity, his pride, and his right to personal security. EB listened, but was still too young to understand the depth of his father's emotion.

The next day, the three boys discussed their punishments, which in all cases were physical and harsh, but not lasting. EB and Matty did not hassle Harold about it. They understood that they were at fault too, for not asking him where he got the money. Harold always had a little money, but thirty dollars was a relative fortune. They should have been more suspicious. Actually they were suspicious, they admitted, but they still kept their mouths shut. That was the mistake. They knew it was wrong, they knew they were wrong, but they went ahead anyway. They were not good at this kind of thing. It was a known fact among Brooklyn kids that Catholics made terrible thieves.

Catholic guilt was a heavy burden.

But for a Catholic kid, the pain of guilt did not last long.

Because there was a sacrament called confession. But confession only complicated things. If a Catholic kid committed a crime on a Wednesday night he was confessing to it by Saturday afternoon. So there was no long range career path in stealing for a Catholic.

Lucky Luciano did not become a crime kingpin by spilling his guts every Saturday afternoon.

Confession eased the pain of the guilt, but that led to an even bigger problem. It was a weird Vatican version of double jeopardy.

After you stole it, you had to give it back.

That was your penance. Recompense, my son.

To get absolution, you had to give recompense.

Stealing without getting caught was difficult enough, but if you were a Catholic kid, you had to do it twice. You had to steal it without getting caught. And you had to give it back without getting caught.

Clearly for EB and most of his friends, a life of crime was too complicated.

Upon due reflection, it seemed to EB that a Catholic thief was an oxymoron.

But they were still kids, and lessons had to be learned over and over again before they stuck.

There was a Woolworth's on Flatbush Avenue where EB, Matty, and Harold did their Christmas shopping. During the rest of the year they visited that particular store infrequently. But in the summer of 1945, they became more interested because they heard the store got in a shipment of plastic World War II warships. The ships were accurate replicas of submarines, destroyers, cruisers, battleships, and aircraft carriers.

They were small, about five inches in length.

Highly prized. And conveniently pocket-sized.

The three boys cruised the store for a week or so, and on each pass of that particular counter managed to come away with a ship or two stuck in a jacket pocket. Before long, they had a collection of two dozen ships that did not cost them a dime.

Then they went to confession. And all three confessed the same sin. And were given the same penance.

Give 'em back, said the priest.

Recompense, my son.

Stealing the ships was easy.

Giving them back was difficult.

They discussed the problem at length and agreed to put all the purloined plastic ships in a paper bag and leave it somewhere in the store where someone would find it.

Good plan.

Now, who would do it? All three of them? No, that would look too suspicious and they'd never get out alive. No, one of them had to do it. Who?

They agreed to choose it up. One or two fingers. One takes it. Odd-man out does the job. "Choose up" among three kids was not the thinking, strategic challenge of one-on-one choosing. Here you couldn't go on tendencies and the psychology of numbers. This was luck. But strategy still played a role. EB figured the odds that Matty and Harold would each throw out the same number of fingers was slight, so he could throw out either a one or two and be home free. Of course Matty and Harold were thinking the same thing.

ONCE, TWICE, SHOOT!

All three boys threw out two fingers.

Amazing.

Now EB figured that either Matty or Harold had to throw out one finger. One of them had to change. Both would not repeat. So if EB threw out a one he couldn't lose.

ONCE, TWICE, SHOOT!

Matty and Harold each repeated with twos.

And EB threw out a one.

Shit!

Oh well, he was the fastest runner and maybe it was better this way. If he had to get out of there fast, he would be a blur.

The Flash.

EB grabbed the paper bag, told the other two boys to wait on the sidewalk and be ready to go in a hurry. He entered one of the main doors and sauntered up the middle aisle. As he walked, he began to feel a little uneasy. He thought everybody was looking at him. Geez, he wondered if he looked guilty. Slow down, he told himself. Everybody in the whole damn store was staring at him. He suddenly wondered if they had a store dick. Those big, burly guys in plainclothes like in a Dick Powell movie who would stalk you, catch you in the act, take you to the back room, and beat the hell out of you. He was starting to sweat. He did not dare look around for the ex-cop dick he was now sure was following him. He reached the rear of the store, turned to the left and started down the aisle where the plastic ship counter was. He quickened his pace even though he knew he shouldn't. They were all on to him now. This stupid paper bag! he whined to himself, it's not a Woolworth bag. It's a dead giveaway! Somebody was going to grab him before he reached the counter.

He was moving faster now.

Panicking now.

Running now.

As he passed the counter, he threw the brown bag filled with stolen plastic ships on top of the World War II warship display and really turned on the speed. He wasn't exactly a blur like the Flash, but he was out of there in a big hurry. As he burst through the door, he shouted to the other two boys to RUN!...and the three of them took off across Flatbush Avenue. They headed toward Avenue H and didn't stop running till they reached 34th Street. There was an empty house there and they hid on the front stoop.

And waited there to see if they were followed.

Of course they weren't followed. Their Big Caper was just a little amusing scene to the sales people in Woolworth's. They were all women, mostly young, and they had seen this before, with variations. The tossed paper bag was a new wrinkle to the women and three or four of them gathered around and giggled as they watched the well-used bag being emptied onto the counter....WELL, THEY LOOK NONE THE WORSE FOR THE WEAR....said the young lady behind the counter as she re-displayed the plastic ships one by one. The little crowd attracted another sales- woman who had witnessed the scene from another aisle and who obviously was new to the store and a non-Catholic to boot.

WHAT THE HECK IS THE REASON FOR THIS?...she asked, holding up the now empty well-used paper bag.

CONFESSION!...said the other four sales ladies in unison.

CONFESSION?...said the only non-Catholic, not quite understanding.

CATHOLIC THIEF...they said, again in unison...DOING HIS PENANCE...

OHHHH...

EB, Matty, and Harold and their friends used the garage roofs, trees, and telephone cables as a kind of aerial highway.

Once they were up there, they could move around pretty good. EB often said that he could travel the length of a block without ever touching solid ground. That was stretching the truth of course, but the sense of it wasn't too far off. They used the trees to get onto some garage roofs, and they used the telephone cables to travel between roofs. Matty and EB did not even need a tree to get onto most roofs. If there were two garages next to each other and their walls were close enough for the two of them to get their backs on one wall and their feet on the other, then they were up in no time. They inched up the wall by moving their backs up a few inches with the feet braced and then bracing the back so the feet could follow. When they reached the roof line, they put one foot on the wall behind them, one foot on the wall in front, straightened as much as possible, put one hand on the back roof, the other hand on the front roof, and swung their bodies onto the front roof. The only garage roof that defeated them was the one that stood alone. And who wanted to be on that, anyway?

On summer nights, they used their aerial highway to check out bedroom windows in hopes of seeing some beautiful young girl undressing for bed. They were an attentive, appreciative, loyal, dependable, highly mobile summer audience that nobody ever knew existed.

But they were out there.

Not every night, but three or four times a month.

And they had their favorite locations.

One was on Brooklyn Avenue between Glenwood Road and Farragut Road. There were two sisters who lived in a big white house in the middle of the block. They were both beautiful. They had separate bedrooms, both in the back of the house. And as luck would have it, there was a cluster of garages in back of their house.

That was a priority stop.

The youngest girl's room was on a bit of an angle from the edge of the roof so you got a better direct view if you hand-over-handed out onto the telephone cable and kind of hung there...just hung there...waiting.

So on a hot summer night, if you wandered into that backyard on Brooklyn Avenue and looked up, you would see four or five dangling shapes hanging there in the dark like a bunch of slacker bats who missed the wake-up call.

Yes, EB, Matty, Harold and other kids were there on summer nights. Sitting on the roof, hanging on the telephone cable, faithful, regular, loyal...but what really made it perverse was that they never saw anything.

Not a damn thing. Ever.

But in their goofy, innocent, naive Catholic way, they were always hopeful and never got discouraged.

5

Chapter Five-The Seasons

In the Flatbush of the '40s, there was a season for every-thing.

Starting in April, it was baseball. That lasted through the summer and included many variations like softball, stickball (one-bounce on the street and fast-pitching against the wall in the schoolyard of PS 198), stoop ball, boxball, and Chinese handball (played against the brick wall of McDade's saloon).

Two-handed touch football started in August and ended when the cold and wind became a problem.

Right before school started in September all the kids got out their roller skates. They were made of steel. The foot pad length was adjustable with a wing nut. The skates clipped onto the soles of the kid's shoes and tightened with a special key that the boy or girl wore on a string around the neck. The wheels were steel, too. They had ball bearings inside arranged in a circle like the cylinders of an aircraft engine. They came spilling out when the kid wore through the outer wheel casing. The wheels basically fell apart because of hard use and the punishment they took from the cracked and craggy Brooklyn streets. Spare wheels were standard equipment.

The kids would lay out chalk trails that would twist and turn halfway down the block then return. Here and there were off-trail rectangles representing rest areas, houses, and a traffic court. The largest such area was a jail. If you were caught by a kid-cop going out of the chalk lines, exceeding the speed limit (very arbitrary...EB loved being a cop), or generally acting in an anti-social manner, you were taken to the traffic court and assigned jail time. The length of time depended on the severity of the offense.

Didn't like your punishment? Thought it was unfair?
Tough.

Take it with good humor or be ostracized...a fate that was truly worse than death.

(There were no adults involved in any of this. Adults played no role in the street life of these kids. Outside of the home, this under-age society was totally self-regulated. And that was true of every aspect of their lives, be it sports, street games, board games, or any form of social intercourse. They made their own rules. And each individual played by those rules. Or didn't play.)

Simple...direct.

The code.

Winter usually brought five or six significant snowfalls. And that meant get out the Flexible Flyers. Everybody had his own sled, and EB was no exception. But EB had a special sled, a secret weapon. It was smaller, lighter, faster, and more maneu-verable than a Flexible Flyer. And he made good use of it. He'd go sledding along the streets, run, bellywhop, ride it out, get up, run, bellywhop, ride it out, and do it all again...all the way down the block. (These kids had to be in good shape.) He'd go sledding in the "woods" with literally hundreds of other kids and, of course, he'd find other less benign and even dangerous uses of snow and sled that only a city kid could conceive of. That kind of sledding he only whispered about among his friends.

When winter faded and the weather warmed, out came the marbles. (Rounds, no dubs, knuckles down.) There were many variations on the game of marbles. All intense. All involving skill, gamesmanship, and smarts.

Basketball was the exception. Basketball had no season. It was played all year in all kinds of weather except hard rain. On ninety-degree days in August or twenty-degree days in January, the game was played. When it snowed, EB and the other kids simply shoveled off the court and played the game.

During the winter, you could always tell a basketball player by looking at the tips of his fingers. They were split and bleeding from handling the wet and freezing basketball.

Those were the seasons. That was the year as lived by EB and his friends. Each season had its own feeling, it own texture. Each year had a predictability and a permanence. And a stability. The repeating pattern was something you could count on...like Brooklyn in the '40s and '50s.

Chapter Six-The Winter 6

A significant winter snowfall brought all the neighbor-hood kids to the "woods". Hundreds of local kids would head there immediately after school or hang out all day on Saturday and Sunday, if that was the timing of the storm.

In the "woods" there was a special hill called "Devil's Ditch". When it snowed it was a hill for the more adventurous kids. So naturally, EB and his cousin Matty spent all their time there.

Devil's Ditch was a an environmentalist's nightmare, the creation of major league erosion forces. It was criss-crossed by wide and deep fissures and foot-deep gullies that followed the downhill line of the hill for its entire hundred-yard length. Some of those cuts would be softened by a good, deep snowfall, but there were two distinctive events as you rode a sled down the hill that no snowfall in the history of weather records could protect you from.

Near the top of the ride, you would fall into a ten foot defile that cut horizontally across the hill. You couldn't avoid it. The sides, although worn, were still mostly straight down. So unless you picked the perfect path, you landed with a thump. And ended your ride. Or splintered your Flexible Flyer.

If you survived that, and most of the kids knew how to traverse the bowl, you picked up speed over a string of relatively benign one-foot moguls and faced your last meaningful challenge. That was an innocent looking little eruption of only about two feet in height. It rose at about a sixty-degree angle, and it was very sneaky because it dipped down directly in front, so it acted like a launching pad. Most kids hit it at speed and went up in the air, ass over tea kettle, lost their sleds, landed on their backsides, or their faces, and slid down the rest of the hill, completing the ride in a very amateurish and humiliating manner.

Not EB and Matty.

To begin with, these two kings of the hill didn't have the mandatory Flexible Flyer. No, these two wiseguys had Mickey Mouse sleds.

Really.

No, really...Mickey Mouse sleds...with portraits of the Mick emblazoned on the body of the sled. Very un-wiseguyish, it would seem. But like everything else these kids valued, these sleds were the tools of the connoisseur. They were strong and smaller by a third than a Flexible Flyer and they were faster and more maneuverable. At age nine or ten, EB and Matty were already too big for these sleds and almost half their bodies hung off the back end, adding to the maneuverability because they could use their legs to steer, drag, or pivot.

Artists.

Taking their turn off the top of Devil's Ditch like the good citizens they were, EB would lead Matty off and drop into the bowl like a Colorado skier carving virgin snow, exit that hazard with much aplomb and increasing speed, and head down toward the dreaded launching pad.

Here is where every kid in the area would stop and watch.

And wonder.

As EB approached the obstacle, he would slip his hands from the steering stick down to the middle of the sled. As he was launched two or three feet into the air, he straightened up, tucked the sled under his arm, and came down on his two feet, gliding to a graceful, ballet-like stop. Then turned and watched Matty repeat the same awesome maneuver. All the kids on that hill agreed on two things.

You couldn't do that on a Flexible Flyer.

And you couldn't do that if you weren't EB and Matty.

Every snowfall was an opportunity for a fight. Snowball fights between individuals, groups, or blocks were routine.

This was a snowball battle between East 40th Street, EB's block, and East 39th, Matty's block. EB was twelve. And on top of his game. He loved the idea of the big battle, a cast of thousands (in his head), deadly projectiles whizzing past his face, guys getting careless and getting whomped and wounded (Medic!!). So on this day he got his block together, kids mostly his own age, Bud Bohan, Ed Overholt, the Mitchells, the manic Rea brothers, maybe fifteen in all, and challenged Matty's block.

Of course, in reality, the fight was not like EB's fantasy. This was not close-in fighting. No hand-to-hand combat here. Each group took its own side of the street, and spread out on the sidewalk. They were usually throwing over piles of shoveled snow across the street to other piles of snow. At best, you could only see the other guys from the head down to the belt buckle. Not much of a target for twelve-year-old arms.

And it didn't remain a pure block-to-block contest for very long. Other kids from other blocks got the word and joined in on both sides. So it got much bigger and much more chaotic, which was OK, but it didn't get much more accurate. So a lot of stuff was flying around without much effect. After a half-hour or so, it started to get a little boring for some kids. Sensing that, EB armed himself with as many snowballs as he could carry and, like a World War I movie, he scampered up out of his sidewalk trench and charged the opposition. Running out into the middle of the street, screaming his semi-Italian curses, he picked his now more exposed targets and expended his ammunition with some good effect. But what he really loved was drawing all that return fire. Every kid on the other side was throwing at him. And mostly missing. He counted on that. Being the wiseguy he was, he knew that if he kept moving, only a lucky shot from those mostly inaccurate arms would get him. After he got off all his snowballs, he zig-zagged back to his own lines, suffering no more than a few glancing blows. Very dramatic, very inspiring. And it kept the game going for a while longer.

As resident wiseguy, that was EB's responsibility.

So he did it again and again.

But inevitably, the interest petered out. And the fight was over. Without a word but in complete agreement, all the kids moved to Glenwood Road and, reaching the corner, turned toward Pease's candy store.

It was about four o'clock in the afternoon in late January, and the descending sun was at their backs. There were a lot of kids, maybe thirty or more, spread out, walking on the sidewalks and on the street.

If you were at Pease's on that winter afternoon in 1946, and if you looked west at their approach, you would have said they blocked out the sun.

Warrior wiseguys.

There was another kind of sleigh riding that EB and his friends did, but didn't talk about except among themselves. And when they did, it sounded like they were telling war stories. Because it was dangerous. And, of course, it was macho so they never mentioned the danger.

And that they were afraid

EB, Matty, and Bob Utter, EB's class-mate from St. Vincent Ferrer, were standing on the sidewalk a little short of the corner of Glenwood Road and Albany Avenue. They were all eleven years old. It had snowed hard and deep a few days before and the streets, still covered with snow, were now burnished to a high, glass-like glaze. It was a cold night in early February. This particular kind of sleigh ride was better enjoyed (if that's the word) at night.

They were on this corner because there was a traffic light there. And they were short of the corner because they did not want to be seen by a motorist who was waiting for a red light. They were looking for one single car stopped for the light with no others behind. When that situation developed, they picked up the sleds at their feet and, staying low, glided out into the street, up to and behind the stopped car. They reached up, grabbed the

44

car's bumper with one hand, spread out across the rear of the car, and waited. If they were lucky (or unlucky), the driver wouldn't notice them sneaking up in his rear view mirror, which is why this worked best at night. And this night it worked just fine.

The car took off; they hung on. Quickly they were skimming across the hard-packed snow at a surprisingly high speed. Their concerns were many but unexpressed.

They were going too fast.

They couldn't see anything, forward or backward. The tires were kicking up snow all over them and, worse, into the faces of EB and Matty, who were on the outside, directly behind the wheels.

If they hit a bump or a snow pile, they could lose their sleds, or (calamity!) if they ran out of snow and hit a bare patch of street, the sled would be ripped out from under them and their legs and stomachs would become the sleds.

(That could be uncomfortable.)

They always worried about another car overtaking them for obvious reasons, but mainly because the guy would blow his horn warning the driver of their car that something was wrong.

On top of all this, they didn't have any idea where the car they were attached to was headed. So on this night, they hung on.

And worried, silently.

Soon enough they realized that the car was headed to Carnarsie. The end of the world. Farms. Italians (who spoke real Italian!), And unpaved roads. Without conversation, they all understood they had to get off. It was possible to communicate, but they had to be careful and speak only in exaggerated whispers so the driver would not hear. So they agreed to abandon the car if and when it stopped for a red light.

It didn't. And they were getting deeper into foreign territory.

EB was on the outside right, so he edged out and took a look. He saw a long straightaway with snow piled high on the side of the road. He looked behind, saw nothing, so he made a quick decision for all of them. He told them on his signal to drop off and glide over to the right. He didn't want to do it under a streetlight, so he waited for a darker spot and gave the word.

They released their grips, coasted over to the side of the road, and glided along the side of the five-foot high snow piles in a single line until they stopped.

And tried to figure out where they were.

As was always the case, an animated, expletive-filled argument followed. But finally they agreed they were somewhere past Remsen Avenue, probably around 93rd Street. About a mile and a half from their neighborhood.

To make matters worse, it had to be close to 9PM. Their parents were pretty easy about being out at night because they thought the kids were hanging out at Pease's candy store. Their parents didn't know about the sleds. If they had, things would have toughened up in a hurry.

EB, Matty, and Bob Utter made a decision and started walking toward what they hoped would be Remsen Avenue. There were no cars in sight on this road, but Remsen Avenue was always busy. They reached it in a few minutes.

They saw a single car stopped for a light and headed in the right direction. They sneaked up on it and grabbed the bumper. The driver opened his window and started screaming at them.

Snagged.

But they didn't move, and wouldn't unless he got out of the car. Sometimes guys yelled and screamed but did nothing. And sometimes drivers knew they were there and went along with it.

Not this guy.

The light changed and he floored it.

Psycho!

The tires spun, spitting up chunks of icy, dirty snow onto the bodies and into the faces of the three kids. When the rear tires reached a small patch of bare pavement, the car lurched forward, skidding left, then right. And throwing off the young hitchhikers.

Some guys were such shitheads.

How stupid was that? They could have gotten hurt, f'God's sake.

Psycho. Geez.

They stood there by the sidewalk, hurting physically from the beating they took from the stinging snow clumps. And hurting psychologically from the defeat at the hands of this adult wiseguy. A wiseguy without a sense of humor. Must have been from Manhattan.

46

Good.

No, bad.

A cop car.

The police car rolled to a stop. The passenger side window rolled down. A gruff, no nonsense voice said...EB?...the voice belonged to Mr. Mitchell, EB's East 40th Street neighbor, patriarch of the Mitchell clan, father of Eddie, coach of EB's baseball team, and one tough son of a bitchin' detective cop from the 69th Precinct in Carnarsie. Silence from EB, head down...WHAT ARE YOU KIDS DOING AROUND HERE THIS TIME OF NIGHT?...NOTHIN', MR. MITCHELL...said EB...SLEIGH RIDING, HUH?...YOU JERKS...ARE YOU IDIOTS HITCHING RIDES ON CARS?...EB considered saying no, but it was not in him to lie to a man like Mr. Mitchell. He was frightening, of course, but that was not it. EB respected him immensely. Besides, Brooklyn wiseguys only lied when they were running a scam. And you didn't scam a man like Mr. Mitchell.

So he said...YES.

Mr. Mitchell responded to the honesty of the answer (he expected nothing less). He quietly told them to put their sleds into the trunk, get into the back seat, and he and his (silent) partner would take them back to Pease's (he would not take them home...he would take them to Pease's...was Mr. Mitchell a sharp guy, or what?).

On the way he chewed out their little asses non-stop. Up, down, backwards and forwards...YES, MR. MITCHELL, NO, MR. MITCHELL, NEVER AGAIN, MR. MITCHELL, YES SIR, NO SIR, ...heads down, contrite, meek, all replying in unison.

And not meaning a word of it.

Standing in front of Pease's, the police car gone, and ready to head home, they all agreed that Mr. Mitchell was one hell of a guy. But they had no intention of paying any attention to Mr. Mitchell lessons of tough love.

They would ride again.

The Mitchells lived at 836 East 40th Street, in the usual semi-detached single family home with a high, two-tiered front stoop. The house was across the street from where EB lived, and down the block, closer to Glenwood Road.

Police officers, even detectives, didn't make a whole lot of money in those days, so in the Mitchell house, money was scarce. Mr. Mitchell and his wife Kathleen had six kids, which didn't help matters. Five were boys. The oldest was Eddie. He was a year older than EB, but the two were very good friends. EB appreciated Eddie's off-beat philosophy of life. In fact, EB loved Eddie Mitchell for being a very interesting half-a-beat off. By the time Eddie was 14 years old, his political positions were fully formed.

Other kids in the neighborhood were convinced that Eddie was a Communist. In that neighborhood at that time, it was not a compliment. EB disagreed (naturally); he viewed Eddie's political beliefs as sophisticated, aware, and for Eddie, extremely rational. Obviously Eddie believed in sharing the wealth because he didn't have any. (EB could relate to that.) Eddie firmly believed in the Welfare State because he was not overly fond of working. He believed in governmental responsibility for the individual because it was a lot more comfortable than taking care of himself. And he believed in free love because it was a hell of a lot easier than the alternative. And easy was the name of Eddie's game.

EB didn't agree with that philosophy, but he couldn't argue the logic of it from Eddie's point of view. Besides, it got everybody else all upset and nuts.

And that was always interesting.

So they were close, and occasionally EB would "call for" Eddie at his house. That did not make EB uncomfortable at all, but on the other hand, there was something about the Mitchell house that did not allow him to feel exactly comfortable, either. It was a very dark house, particularly in the winter. But the odd thing about it was the fact that there was never anyone around, even with all those kids. It was usually deserted except for Mrs. Mitchell. She was always there.

It was a year after the hitchhiking incident, and on this winter afternoon, EB rang the bell of the Mitchell house and waited. One of the little kids, Charlie, opened the door and asked him in, told him he'd tell Eddie EB was there, and disappeared. EB walked into the darkened living room. Mrs. Mitchell was in the kitchen ironing. Mrs. Mitchell was always in the kitchen ironing. Night or day, it seemed, she ironed. She called out a greeting to EB (she was a very soft, pretty, kind, and gracious woman, like most of the mothers on the block) and went back to her ironing.

EB slumped into the first chair he saw, sat quietly, and waited, which seemed like the thing you did in the Mitchell house. EB stayed quiet as he looked around the room. Then, as his eyes became more accustomed to the half light, he became aware that there was a figure lying on the slightly faded, over-stuffed sofa facing him. It was Mr. Mitchell. He was curled on the soft seat cushions with his red-suspendered back to EB, his face turned, buried in the sofa's cushioned backrest. EB heard a few snores and didn't dare move, afraid to awaken the big detective.

Eddie's voice floated down from somewhere upstairs and announced that he was on his way down. EB answered with a quiet grunt.

At this point, Mr. Mitchell turned and faced EB.

HOW Y'DOIN, EB?...he said, sleepily.

He had a lighted cigar in his mouth.

EB sat there, staring at that cigar, zeroed in on that glow-ing tip, flicked a glance at Eddie bounding down the stairs, and didn't bat an eye.

Standard Operating Procedure. Nothing surprised him in this house, in this neighborhood.

That same winter, in February, it snowed heavily. About fourteen or fifteen inches. EB was in eighth grade. On his way to school at eight fifteen in the morning. He was one of first people out this early in the morning.

St. Vincent Ferrer almost never closed in the '40s. And if it did, you had to go there to find out. It would never be announced in advance.

EB left his house and started walking up the block toward Glenwood Road. He was walking down the center of the street. That's what you did when there was a significant snowfall. That made it seem more like New England to EB. On days like this he made believe he lived in Connecticut or Vermont.

It was still snowing and blowing up big drifts as EB made his way up the block. He was leaving the only tracks in the street. Virgin snow. EB loved it. There were few cars on the move dur-ing a storm like this, and not many cars parked along the curb. Cars were not that ubiquitous then. EB's family did not own one, and his parents did not know how to drive. It was not that unusual in this working-class neighborhood. As EB reached mid-block, he became aware of a strange car parked in front of the Mitchell's house. There was something odd about it that he couldn't put his finger on. He then remembered that Mr. Mitchell bought a new car a couple of weeks before. Not a new car, exactly. Used. But new for them. And the kids were excited about it. But that was not it.

There was something else. A visual thing that was confusing, strange.

As EB got closer, he got it.

There was a lovely snowdrift that began on the Mitchell's high front lawn and swept down in an elegant unbroken line to a point in middle of the street that EB now approached.

But the odd thing was that the Mitchell car was directly in the path of that elegant line...yet the line was unimpeded. Uninterrupted.

A quirk of nature?

No, a quirk of the Mitchells

The night before, the family, (the little kids probably), had neglected to close the rear car windows...any of the rear windows.

All of the rear windows were open.

As EB trudged past, he saw that the rear seat of the car was filled with snow, supporting that beautiful drift that began on the elevated lawn and ran right through the car to the street.

EB smiled.

He loved his block. He loved the Mitchells. He loved all his neighbors. He loved his neighborhood.

Chapter Seven-The Summer **7**

The "woods" was doomed.

There wasn't enough time or space for a Sherwood Forest anymore. The mid-twentieth century had no patience for it. It was a void. It had to be filled. It was unused; it was unprofitable.

It was un-American.

"Build it up," they said (tear it down).

"Develop it," they said (make it disappear).

"Rescue it," they said (kill it).

And so they did. But not all at once. That's not the way they do things. "Progress" happens slowly, in stages. They're smart that way.

So around 1940, they began to build single-family brick homes in the east end of the "woods," on the blocks between 37th Street and 41st Steet (Albany Avenue). And from Farragut Road to Foster Avenue.

But they were even smarter than smart.

They also began to build a park.

Paerdegat Park.

It was downright diabolical. The kids didn't know how to feel. They hated to lose their special place, but gosh, a park, with softball fields, basketball courts, swings, monkey bars, handball courts, even a picnic area. Geez, what confusion; how are you supposed to feel?

EB knew how he felt, even at age seven.

He hated it.

And during the year it took to finally complete the park, he and some of the older kids from the neighborhood turned into urban guerrillas. After the workmen left at four o'clock in the afternoon, the kids would arrive and try to undo everything the workers did that day. They knocked over the still-wet beginnings of brick walls; they overturned buckets, barrels, and stacked two-by-fours; they knocked over anything they could budge. They broke window frames and door frames, and later, they broke windows. They broke anything that would break. They did all they could but, of course, it was not enough.

By 1941, the park was built.

And by 1945 ,they had completely stolen the whole section of the "woods" from 40th to 36th Streets and from Farragut to Foster. The homes they built there were known as the Trump Homes. (Yes, the father of that Trump.) But the kids still had "Devil's Ditch" and the ball fields and the rest of the "woods" down to Nostrand Avenue. And they would have all of that until about 1950, when it all disappeared.

Literally, paradise lost.

But as it turned out, for EB, the park was the best thing that ever happened. As he got older, he spent all his time there. Playing every kind of game there was to play...softball, basketball, football, handball, stickball, and running, jumping, leaping, hanging, and swinging...sculpting his body, honing his skills.

In a neighborhood of good ballplayers, even great ballplayers, EB was discovering he could hold his own — hold his own with kids that lived on his own block, with kids in his own neighborhood, and even with kids who traveled from other neighborhoods to play in Paerdegat Park.

EB played on two organized baseball teams from ages twelve to fourteen. One was St. Vincent Ferrer's grammar school team, which belonged to the CYO League. He played second base. The "Cardinals" was the other team; it belonged to a more loosely organized independent league. He played shortstop on that team.

One day during the season of 1947, the Cardinals played a doubleheader and EB went seven for eight, including a home run, a triple, two doubles, and three singles. He stole home on the second pitch after his triple. He drove the other team nuts that day (his mission in life).

Undoubtedly, that was his finest day as a baseball player.

And just as undoubtedly, from a baseball point of view, EB peaked at the age of twelve.

On another day of that same season in early summer of 1947, he was playing second base for St. Vincent Ferrer. He went oh for three in that game. But his first time up, he walked, stole second, stole third, and scored on an infield ground ball to the left side (normally a no-no, but EB was faster than no-no's).

And that's why Mr. Mitchell, his coach, loved him.

Even when he didn't hit, he still made things happen. EB never stopped. If he hit the ball through the infield, he thought "double" and ran full-tilt from the crack of the bat. Sometimes he took the extra base, sometimes he couldn't, but he always thought that way. His aggressive base running put big-time pressure on the opposing team's fielders, and often they couldn't handle it. They were, after all, just twelve year old kids.

On that day, sitting next to Mr. Mitchell on the bench was his good friend, Mr. Fogarty. "Pop" Fogarty they called him. The neighborhood legend was that Mr. Fogarty was a former minor league ball player. He was a gruff, intimidating, big man with a pronounced ruddy complexion. To EB, his face always looked like it was about to explode.

Fogarty had a son named Joseph. He was a year and a half behind EB in ST. Vincent Ferrer. He had a building reputation as a good athlete. EB knew that, knew Joe casually, and liked him.

But Mr. Fogarty didn't like EB.

EB WAS TOO AGGRESSIVE. (Just like Mr. Fogarty.)

EB WAS TOO ARROGANT. (Just like Mr. Fogarty.)

EB WAS A WISEGUY. (No further comment.)

Around the seventh inning of this particular game, the batter hit a slow, nicely bouncing ground ball right at EB. He moved in, bobbled it, recovered frantically, and just barely threw the kid out.

From the St. Vincent Ferrer bench came a stream of invective. Sort of like clean curses. No dirty words, but just as intimidating.

WHADDYA THINK YER DOIN' KID...KEEP YOUR GLOVE DOWN...DON'T BE SCARED OF THE BALL...KEEP YOUR HEAD DOWN...MOVE...CHARGE THE BALL...MAKE THE PLAYS...Y'GOT STONE HANDS OR SOMETHING?...GET YOUR HEAD IN THE GAME, KID...WHERE D'YA THINK YOU ARE?...BALLET SCHOOL?

This, of course, was not Mr. Mitchell.

In the years EB knew Mr. Mitchell as a man, a coach, a father, a neighbor, he never heard him talk to a kid like that. Mr. Mitchell was a tough cop, but he was too smart a coach, too good a coach, and too good a man to chew a kid out for a mechanical error. (Actually, since the batter was ultimately out at first, technically there was no error. The only "E" you got for a play like that was a small "e" for embarrassment.) From his second base position, EB saw Mr. Mitchell look at Fogarty, but no words were exchanged.

Naturally, as always happens in baseball, the next batter hit another ground ball right at EB. Not a tough chance at all.

Routine.

EB blew it big-time. Kicked it, picked it up, dropped it, picked it up again, and threw it in the dirt in front of the first baseman.

Rattled.

A mortal sin for a Brooklyn wiseguy. He'd let the old guy get to him.

Shit.

Again Mr. Fogarty let loose with a decidedly hostile stream of baseball trash-talk, but louder this time. Mr. Mitchell, God bless him, cut him off quick and clean.

SHUT UP, NOBODY TALKS TO MY BOYS EXCEPT ME...I'M THE COACH...YOU'RE THE GUEST...ACT LIKE IT, DAMMIT...WHAT THE HELL'S WRONG WITH YOU?...THE

KID MADE AN ERROR...YOU REMEMBER THOSE DON'T YOU?...YOU OUGHT TO, YOU SURE MADE ENOUGH OF 'EM IN YOUR TIME...NOW SHUT UP OR GET THE HELL OUT OF HERE.

Then shouting out to EB...OK, SHAKE IT OFF, DON'T WORRY ABOUT IT. PLAY BALL.

But EB couldn't shake it off and did worry about it.

Yeah, he was a wiseguy, but he was also twelve years old.

Fast forward one month to a very hot, mid-summer day, 1947. It was about eleven-thirty in the morning and already very close to ninety degrees. EB was on the basketball court at Paerdegat Park. He'd been playing basketball for two and a half hours. Three-man, half-court games. Six baskets win. Serious games. Smart games. Heady games. Blood games. Lose and get off the court and wait for "winners". There were fifteen or twenty kids waiting, so there could be as many as five or six three-man teams in front of you. The kids who had "winners" had already chosen their teammates, but occasionally they would hold one spot open so they had the option of picking a kid from the losing team. That was the rule, although it didn't happen that often. After a loss then, the wait tended to be long.

So the idea was not to lose.

EB was on the court when Buddy Bohan showed up and insisted that they had to talk.

Buddy...Francis "Red" Bohan...lived a few doors away from EB on 40th Street and was one of his oldest friends. Buddy was two years younger with crew-cut orange-red hair and a body that was lean and lanky. Skinny, actually. He had worn thick, horn-rimmed glasses for as long as EB could remember. EB used him for jujitsu practice when they were younger (learned from watching John Wayne movies), but now Buddy was growing taller and stronger and no longer stood for that kind of humiliation.

Despite that seemingly unimpressive physical description, Buddy was a superior, well-coordinated athlete and a tough competitor.

And a loyal and good friend.

He was also EB's agent (unpaid, of course).

Which explained this unwelcome interruption.

Business, of a kind.

EB called time, got another kid to take his place, and pulled Buddy aside. His friend informed him that "Pop" Fogarty was outside on the softball field and was challenging EB to a three hundred yard race against his son, Joe.

ARE YOU INSANE?...THAT'S NO CONTEST...JOE CAN'T RUN WITH ME, I'LL BEAT THE HELL OUT OF HIM...I DON'T WANT TO DO THAT IN FRONT OF HIS FATHER...NO MATTER WHAT KIND OF SON OF BITCH THE OLD MAN IS...GO OUT THERE AND TELL POP FOGARTY I WON'T RACE...TELL HIM IT'S TOO HOT...TELL HIM I HAVE A FEVER...TELL HIM YOU COULDN'T FIND ME...TELL HIM ANYTHING YOU WANT, BUT TELL HIM TO GO HOME...NO RACE, NO WAY.

Buddy left for the softball field.

EB returned to his basketball game. But even before he could get the kid who took his place out of the game (negotiations, always negotiations) and get back in himself, Buddy was back.

FOGARTY SAYS YOU'RE A CHICKEN SHIT.

That did it.

EB walked (sauntered?) out onto the softball field. He was dressed in a white tee shirt and just-starting-to-fade Levi's, three sizes too long and rolled up at the cuff so that the inner, dark blue seam could be seen. Very fashionable at the time. On his feet were well-worn white Chuck Taylor hightops over two sets of woolen sweat socks. He and his clothes were soaked in sweat from the basketball battles.

As he approached the two boys and Mr. Fogarty, he kept his eyes on Buddy only. He couldn't...wouldn't...look at Pop Fogarty. Or his son. He knew that he was coming across as incredibly arrogant, probably insulting, but he couldn't help himself. He was sincerely pissed at Pop Fogarty.

He asked what the rules were, again looking only at Bohan. He quickly agreed and started toward the starting line, sizing up Joe Fogarty as he walked (sauntered?). The kid was wearing racing shorts and a kind of basketball shirt with straps and no sleeves. His sneakers were the same brand as EB's, but low cut. He was dressed for a race. He looked cool and sleek and fast, like a silver P-51 Mustang. This was an outfit no doubt insisted upon by his cunningly agressive father.

How embarrassing.

They stood at the starting line and Joey immediately got down in a racer's three point stance.

Unbelievable!

EB stood there, casual as you please, and for the first time looked at the old man...COUNT IT DOWN...he barked. As Fogarty started counting, EB looked down at Joey and rolled his eyes. Joey smiled slightly, and the two kids understood each other. It was worked out. The subtle, more important game within the game was agreed to and it was the only game that counted.

The race started.

And ended at the start.

EB got out in front fast and stayed there as the two boys raced around the periphery of the softball field. He was not pushed, and at the end he was a comfortable five yards ahead of Joe Fogarty.

EB crossed the finish line and kept going.

He didn't say a word, he didn't look back, he just kept going...back to the basketball courts he had come from...arrogant as hell but he figured it was the ultimate insult to a man who was trying so hard to get to him that he'd humiliate his own son to do it. EB was fully aware that this was his opportunity for revenge against Mr. Fogarty, but he didn't feel very good about using Joe Fogarty as the vehicle. He also knew he could have tripled his lead and devastated the other kid. The fact that he didn't, and didn't want to, made him feel good.

As he jogged away, he heard old man Fogarty chewing out his son. Screaming at him, demeaning his own child. Geez, what an asshole.

But it was a lesson learned.

EB vowed then and there that if he was ever going to be a father, he would not be a father like Mr. Fogarty.

Pop Fogarty didn't get it.

But right then...right there...EB did get it.

There was a time to be a wiseguy...

and there was a time to be a wise guy.

Summer was always the best time in EB's life. He and his friends crammed forty-eight hours of living into every twenty four. There was no television to waste time on, and the only radio worth listening to was Martin Block's "Make Believe Ballroom" on Saturday morning. So they spent the days, and the nights, out on the streets, in the park, in the "woods", at the beach, or at the neighborhood pool (the wondrous Atlantic Ocean and the legendary Farragut Pool). They spent the days in shifting groups...boys, girls, all ages, all sizes, groups of five, ten, fifteen, twenty. Kids came and left, other kids took their places; everybody was welcome. It depended on what was going on at the moment. Kids had their individual strengths and interests and family obligations, so they were there when they wanted to be or could be. They played the national games and they played the Brooklyn games. They played baseball, basketball, softball, handball, stoopball, stickball, boxball. They played Kick the Can, "War", Hide and Seek, Johnny-Ride-the-Pony, and Red Rover. They chose up sides and played "guns". (Their version of World War II movies. Thirty kid-commandos scrambling for cover behind stoop railings, bushes, or tree trunks, shooting imaginary bullets at each other with wooden or plastic replicas of Colt 45's, Lugers, or M-1's, accompanied by a cacophony of imaginative "ricocheting bullet" sounds. When you were obviously "dead" and couldn't get away with arguing the point, you "died" spectacularly...spinning, falling, rolling, clutching your chest, and making weird noises.)

Organized chaos.

They played on their own blocks or traveled to other blocks. When it got dark, they played "Ring-o-livio," or they sat on stoops under streetlights and played Black Jack or Poker for pennies. When it rained, they used the sheltered front porches to play Monoply, checkers, Chinese checkers, Parcheesi and all kinds of card games. They did everything together. When personal problems arose, they were calmly talked over and solved; when arguments broke out, they were allowed to take their course, then arbitrated; when the rules needed to be articulated, and agreed upon, they were.

And not an adult in sight.

As often as they could, they traveled down to the

"beach". EB loved the ocean. When he and Matty were very young, they had to rely on adults to get them there. Riis Park (what they meant when they said "beach") was at the western end of the Rockaway peninsula and a little over six miles from the neighborhood. In the early years, they rode in Matty's family car, or took the Green Bus Line. The bus left from Flatbush Avenue and always had a long line of families waiting for it. Later, from age twelve onward, they were on their own. Then they begged rides with older kids with cars (very rare) or hitched a ride with strangers. More than once, when they couldn't get a ride, they walked it. They wouldn't be caught dead on the bus. They were now much too sharp for that.

Riis Park was located in the borough of Queens. The Rockaway peninsula was connected to the Brooklyn mainland by the Marine Park Bridge. Which, in essence, was the southern terminus of Flatbush Avenue. The middle of the bridge was the dividing line between Brooklyn and Queens. Officially, Riis Park might have been in Queens, but everybody in EB's neighborhood thought of it as "their beach". (Queens? Naaah! It was a Brooklyn beach.)

In their teen years, EB and his friends always got a jump on the summer season. They started to go down to the beach as early as possible; on scattered days in late April if the weather cooperated, every weekend starting in early May. By the official opening of the summer season on the Memorial Day Weekend, they were all tanned up and ready to resent the hordes of "snowbirds" who then descended upon their beach.

(This is how they tanned: get a bad sunburn over your entire body, suffer through the pain till about late Wednesday, see your skin start to peel on Thursday, feel much better by Friday, go back to the beach on Saturday, and do it all over again. You had to get two sunburns! It was in the book! No other way! It did work. But it is a medical miracle that they didn't die of monstrous melanomas by age twenty-five.)

They all loved the ocean. The bigger the surf, the better. They all swam well, rode the waves well, and plunged into, over, and under the breakers with zest, strength, and confidence.

Athletes.

As usual, everything was a contest. Riding waves was the liveliest competition. The winner (temporarily) was the kid who could ride a wave the longest or the farthest (if you scraped your nose on the sand high on the beach where the water was about two inches deep, you were in the running).

They were comfortable and at home in the ocean, but still, things happened.

One afternoon in late August 1947, EB, Matty, Bobby Waegelein and two other friends, Jerry Frost and Billy Janson, were heading into the ocean at Riis Park. It was about three o'clock in the afternoon. The tide was at low ebb and there was a sandbar about one hundred yards from shore. That's where the breakers were.

The sandbar created a sort of lake between the natural shore line and its front edge. To get out to the sandbar, the five boys waded out a ten or so yards till the water reached shoulder height, then swam the remaining ninety yards to the beginning of the bar. The water they swam over was probably eight to ten feet deep and very still, protected as it was from the breaking, roiling ocean waves.

The front edge of the sandbar was sharply sloping, so you kind of felt for it with your feet before you trusted that you had reached a bottom. Once there, you walked a few feet up the slope to water that was knee deep. Seaward from there, the bar stayed level for another fifty yards. It was as if some mischievous ocean god decided overnight to move the beach one hundred and fifty yards out to sea.

At high tide, the sandbar disappeared. And you never knew if it would return at the next low tide. One of the mysteries of the ocean.

The boys swam out in a group; EB, Matty, and Bobby leading with Billy and Jerry trailing. The first three reached the front edge, touched down, and took a few steps out onto the sandbar. Billy Janson followed, but Jerry Frost miscalculated his distance. He assumed he was there and put both feet down.

And sank like a stone.

He came up...surprised, sputtering.

And began to go down again.

The other four boys jumped back in and hauled him onto the sandbar.

He was flustered, he was coughing up what seemed like

five gallons of salty, fishy sea water, and he was a little embarrassed. And very shook. The boys talked it over (as they always did) and decided to stay on the sandbar long enough for Jerry to relax a little and then head back in.

For half an hour or so, the five of them rode waves on the sandbar. Jerry did his best to join in with some enthusiasm but didn't quite make it believable.

He was worried. And secretly, so was EB.

What was once a crowded sandbar was now practically their private beach. It was getting late, the water on the sandbar was now up to their bathing suits and the waves were running across the sandbar into the "lake", so the tide was coming in. And when tides come in, sandbars go out, or under, or somewhere only the gods know about.

They caucused. And agreed to go.

Jerry was reluctant.

Understandably, he was not feeling very confident in his ability to swim that now-choppy hundred yards of unwelcoming sea water. He could still taste it, and every time he thought about it, he almost gagged.

A serious situation.

At that point, Bobby Waegelein took charge. He went prone into the now three-foot-deep water, told Jerry to sit on his back, and told EB, Matty, and Billy Janson to swim surrounding him all the way in.

Then he pushed off the sandbar and butterflied all the way into shore.

He did the butterfly for a hundred yards with a kid on his back!

He was fifteen years old!

Amazing.

As the years passed and EB thought about this, he could hardly believe he witnessed it. It was the most heroic thing he had ever seen. Bobby was a champion swimmer for St. Francis High School. His specialty was backstroke.

But that didn't explain anything.

The physicality of it...the self-sacrifice of it...the love of it...couldn't easily be explained. And they didn't try. They only knew that this experience drew them closer. It was friendship that no longer needed explanations. To EB, Bobby Waegelein was a real, honest-to-goodness, goddamned hero.

But of course he couldn't tell him that.

Not then.

Chapter Eight-Summer/The Dodgers and Ebbets Field **8**

The Brooklyn Dodgers were a vital part of the texture of summer in EB's neighborhood. And, of course, Ebbets Field was a shrine. That's a cliché, but like a lot of clichés, it was also very true. All the kids lived and died with the Dodgers. They bled Dodger blue (as Tommy LaSorda was later to say).

EB's first real memory of Ebbets Field was in 1946 when his older cousin Bob Campbell, just returned from the Navy and needing to get back in touch with his life, took EB, EB's father, and Bob's own father (Uncle Rob) to a Dodger-St. Louis Cardinal game. It was one of those perfect, bright, sunny days in June, and the stadium was absolutely packed.

Which is one of the reasons the family had no seats.

They actually sat on the concrete steps in the upper stands in the left field corner, (Nice seats, Bob. Ever hear of advanced reserved seating?) And nobody minded. There were fans sitting in all of the aisles, standing in the back, and crowded and crunched into any empty space they could find. The capacity of Ebbets Field was thirty-three thousand, but there must have been close to forty thousand Brooklynites jammed into the place on that day. No problem; the crowd was genial, happy to be there. All the guys were home from the war. The world was at peace. Brooklyn was happy. Even though the Dodgers were getting killed single-handedly by Stan Musial. Musial must have gone five for six that day, and all of his hits were doubles off the right field scoreboard.

BAM, BAM...LADIES AND GENTLEMEN, THE NEXT BATTER IS STAN MUSIAL...BAM, BAM, BAM...

When Musial approached the plate for his last at-bat for the day, the Brooklyn fans gave him a standing ovation.

A standing ovation! Even though he killed them all by himself!

The code.

Brooklyn wiseguys in action; EB loved every minute of it. He was eleven years old and absolutely in awe of it.

By the 1947 season, EB and his cousin Matty inserted Ebbets Field into their normal summer routine. Two or three times a month they would take the Nostrand Avenue or the Rogers Avenue trolley to the ballpark. They'd hang around the rotunda and look small and poor and waifish. They were hoping some adult with extra tickets would feel sorry for them. And sometimes it worked. But not always perfectly.

One day, they were running this scam when a man dressed in a business suit approached them with the possibility of a ticket. One ticket. He was in town from Philadelphia, his business guest was late, he doubted he would show and if that was the case, he would take one of the boys into the game. EB and Matty immediately went to the ticket taker and begged and pleaded to be allowed to sit in one seat.

TWO LITTLE KIDS COULD EASILY FIT INTO ONE SEAT...AND WHAT'S THE HARM...WE WOULDN'T TAKE UP ANY MORE ROOM THAN ONE ADULT...WE'D SIT STILL... WOULDN'T BOTHER ANYBODY...WE'D BE LOW, EASY TO SEE OVER...C'MON GIVE US A BREAK...Y'GOT KIDS OF

YOUR OWN?...WE'D DO IT FOR YOU...NOBODY WOULD MIND... EVERYBODY LIKES KIDS...C'MON, PUULEEESSE?

To no avail.

So they agreed to "choose-it-up." Odds and evens, two out of three throws takes it. On the first throw, EB shouted "odds", and threw out one finger. Matty threw out two fingers. EB won. The next throw, Matty shouted "evens" and threw out two fingers. EB threw out two fingers. Matty won. On the final throw EB shouted "even" and threw out two fingers, Matty did the same, thinking EB would never believe he'd throw three twos in a row (definitely a game of strategy). EB won.

As much as he hated to leave his cousin, the "choose-up" was fair and square, so EB went into the game with the businessman from Philadelphia. Who turned out to be a very nice guy. He bought EB hot dogs, sodas and peanuts and listened politely as EB told him everything he never really wanted to know about the Brooklyn Dodgers.

And he did one more thing for EB. That was the first time EB ever laid eyes on Jackie Robinson.

The kids in EB's neighborhood didn't know what to make of Jackie Robinson. At the beginning, they were against him because he upset the status quo. He was definitely different. He sure looked different. They didn't know a whole lot about Negroes (remember, it was 1947), but they recognized that this was the beginning of something new and they weren't sure what that something was. Jackie Robinson himself seemed somehow threatening.

So they didn't like him, and didn't want him.

That didn't last long.

It took just a month or so of watching Robinson play the game of baseball for the kids and for Brooklyn as a whole to change their minds. When Pee Wee Reese put his arm around Robinson's shoulder in Cincinnati in the face of a murder threat and a stream of brutal racist taunts from some of the Reds players, that was Brooklyn's arm. It was Brooklyn's embrace.

After you felt Robinson's competitive fire, after you witnessed the intensity of his desire to win and his fierce refusal to lose, after you were thrilled by his aggressive base-running, you knew he belonged in Brooklyn.

The kids saw it almost right away...Jackie Robinson was a Brooklyn wiseguy.

He belonged.

It was made in Heaven.

The code worked in mysterious ways.

There was another way to see Robinson and the rest of the Dodgers for free. If you did it right, there was no "choose-up" necessary. You all got in. And you didn't have to depend on the generosity of strangers. You only had to depend on yourself and your athletic ability.

It was easy and straightforward. All you had to do was climb the left field wall of Ebbets Field, using door frames and window sills to reach a narrow ledge on the grandstand level, and inch out hand-over-hand and foot-over-foot for about seventy-five feet to escape an iron fence with overhanging, curved, pointed barbs. Once getting to that point, all you had to do was leap a small fence, sneak over to the men's bathroom, climb to the roof, and hide there until game time when you could come down relatively unnoticed, mingle with the crowd and hopefully find an empty seat.

Easy.

To make this little game even more interesting, you only had a small window of time to work in. If you were too early (before eleven o'clock for a day game), there was nobody in the stands and you were too conspicuous; and if you were too late (eleven forty-five at the latest), the park police were coming on duty and you were dead.

To complicate this just a little further, this was Brooklyn, New York. That means for every home game there were a hundred wiseguys waiting at the base of the left field wall for that little window of time to open.

The line was usually long and the time was always short.

On a day in July 1948, three kids were standing on McKeever Place at the base of the Ebbets Field left field wall.

Arguing.

They were EB, Matty, and Bobby Waegelein (the Johnny Weismuller of Flatbush and now one of EB's true and lasting friends). They were arguing about time. It was about eleven- fif-

66

teen and there were kids scattered all over the wall. Did they have the time?

The wall was clearing, at least on the lower levels, so they quickly agreed to go for it. EB went first, then Matty, then Bobby. They were feeling the time pressure, but they dared not get careless. At the grandstand level, it was about twenty feet straight down. If you fell, you landed on cold, hard sidewalk.

That could hurt.

EB was nearing the halfway point when one of the kids in front of him almost slipped and was now in a state of panic. He wouldn't move. His friends on the wall and on the sidewalk were screaming at him, urging him to get a grip on himself. His friends who were higher were trying to come back to him. What they were going to do when they reached him, EB had no idea. The only thing he knew for sure was that he was hung up on the wall and time was running out. But he couldn't do anything about it, so he hung there. As did Matty and Bobby.

There they were when a group of three cops, just coming on duty, turned the corner off Sullivan Place and headed up McKeever.

All the kids on the sidewalk took off. The panicked kid on the wall almost had a heart attack. EB tried to calm him down, reassuring him that nothing seriously bad would happen. The cops just wanted them off the wall. As for EB, he just kind of hung there and smiled to himself. This was a very familiar situation.

Nailed.

When the cops reached them, they didn't say a word. Just stood there and looked up. Waiting.

The kids who were higher up at the iron fence continued that way. Either they made it all the way into the park or there were cops waiting for them up there. EB never knew as he and Matty and Bobby inched their way down the wall (coming down was a lot harder than going up because you had to find the holds with your feet instead of your hands). When they finally reached the sidewalk, the cops just kept them corralled together. Then they talked the panicked kid down. When the wall was clean of kids, the cops took their little band of desperadoes (about seven kids) around the corner to Montgomery Street, chewed them out, lectured them, whacked them on the backs of the head, and told them to go home.

These police officers were New York City cops, not specials. They all had a lot of Mr. Mitchell in them. Mostly good guys. Fathers, brothers, and city kids themselves, they understood that these were basically good kids. They also understood the psychology (or pathology) of the neighborhood.

Put a system, any system, in front of a Brooklyn wiseguy and he'll try to beat it. It was his sworn duty.

And it was the duty of the system (the cops) to discourage that kind of thing.

With no hard feelings on either side.

EB's loyalty to the Dodgers never wavered. He suffered through the playoff game with the St. Louis Cardinals in 1946. He never forgot the intense pain and the disappointment when Howie (High Howie) Shultz struck out to end the game and give the Cardinals the pennant.

They lost in '46, but that was the beginning of the dynasty.

For the next ten years, the Dodgers were one of the great teams in baseball history. They didn't win the pennant every year but they came close. They won in '47, '49, '52, '53, '55, and '56. And when they won the pennant, they always faced the New York Yankees in the World Series and they always lost (except for 1955 — when the baseball gods finally relented).

The Dodger teams must have been the inspiration for the ABC Sports theme: "The thrill of victory, the agony of defeat." With a definite emphasis on agony.

Yes, sometimes it was hard being a Dodger fan.

But it was a love affair.

And needed no further explanation.

Pete Reiser was EB's hero when he was a little kid. But after '48, Reiser was gone and EB's idols were Reese, Robinson, Snider, Hodges, Campanella, Erskine, Newcombe, Branca, and Furillo. Especially Furillo. EB was very impressed with the way Furillo played the game. A lunch pail guy. A dogged, dependable professional. A pro's pro.

EB admired Furillo a great deal.

He admired them all. From '50 to '56, EB firmly believed that the Dodgers were the best team in all of major league baseball.

And to hell with the Yankees.

The most significant thing about both the Dodger and the Yankee teams, and for that matter all of the other major league teams of that era, was that they were true teams.

In every sense of that word.

For all of those ten years between '47 and '57, the Dodger personnel hardly changed. The eight starters and the nucleus of the pitching staff were the Dodgers you knew and loved. The players did not change every year. Reese was the shortstop today and he'd be the shortstop tomorrow. Robinson and Hodges and Snider and Furillo would be there today. And five years from today. And ten years from today.

The Dodger players lived in the neighborhoods, they traveled to the ballpark in the subways and on the trolleys. They didn't make much more money than some of the kids' fathers. They were a part of Brooklyn. They belonged to Brooklyn. Day in, day out, year after year, the Dodgers were the Dodgers, the Yankees were the Yankees, the Giants were the Giants.

Dependability. Familiarity. Constancy. Consistency. Loyalty. Those words defined the major league ball clubs of the era. Those words defined the decades of the '40s and '50s.

9

Chapter Nine-Summer/The Ladies' Man

EB was not a ladies' man.

It wasn't that he didn't want to be...he loved women...girls, that is. He loved the way they looked (he secretly considered himself a connoisseur), he loved the way they moved, he loved the way they stayed still, he loved the way they smiled. He loved their eyes, their lips, their hair, their legs. He loved them in almost every way.

But he didn't understand how to communicate those feelings, so he was intimidated.

The truth is, girls scared the bejesus out of EB.

He was uncomfortable, ill at ease, not confident in their presence, a feeling he was not used to in most other areas of his life. So he avoided them in an obvious way...and then regretted it. He pretended not to care...and then moaned to himself that nobody (no girl) cared for him.

Contradictory behavior to be sure.

He blamed that on the nuns.

A woman's body was God's temple, the mysterious abiding place of the Holy Ghost, the nuns taught the boys (and taught the boys...and taught the boys). Eight years of that had its effect on EB and most of his friends. A woman was sacred, so you approached her with reverence and respect and humility.

Tough duty for a wiseguy.

So that was the boy-girl situation as EB entered his teenage years. Not all that promising, but certainly not hopeless. EB had been told by enough girls (and boys) that he was a reasonably good-looking guy. One young lady told him he looked like Tom Drake (see..."Meet Me in St. Louis"). Another girl told him he looked like John Derek (see...Bo).

So that wasn't it.

No, it was not his looks; it was him. The arrogance that served him well in other aspects of his life hurt him in the delicate, sensitive, give and take of teenage romance.

He was all take and no give.

To protect the too-fragile, underdeveloped boy-girl aspect of his ego, EB always waited for the girl to commit herself first. So that meant that in most cases, he waited for commitments that never came (after all, the nuns talked to the girls, too).

Checkmate.

But there were moments.

EB's class at St. Vincent Ferrer had a steady cast of forty-five boys and girls, split almost fifty-fifty. (There were a few more boys.) EB had a permanent crush, sometimes long-range, sometimes up-close and personal, with the most beautiful girl in his class...Jenny O'Halloran. She was a classic blonde, blue-eyed beauty right out of central casting. Petite, with lovely translucent white skin and a sensuous, enticing, athletic body. She mesmerized him. They were in the same class for all eight years of grammar school, and to make it more intense for EB, Jenny lived on Matty's block, so they grew up together on the street as well as in the classroom. EB had loved her for as long as he could remember.

But of course, he never told her that, at least not that openly and directly and honestly.

Theirs was an innocent on-again, off-again kid love affair. When they were on, he would stare at her for hours across the classroom. When they were off, he was insanely jealous of every boy in the class who made a move toward her. Eventually, because the other guys were not blind, that love-sick enmity was directed at almost every boy in the class. He glared, he threatened, and when he had to, he fought (kid fights, nobody ever got hurt). But the only kids he scared off were the fat guys and the nerds. The ones who knew they didn't have a shot anyway.

The nuns must have been aware of all this (the nuns were aware of everything), but it was never mentioned.

When they were about eleven or twelve and continuing till maybe fourteen, Jenny came up with a birthday gift idea that EB wholeheartedly endorsed. On or near his birthday in early July, they would meet in the Glenwood Theatre (sic) or the Farragut Movie (sic) and she would give him a kiss for every year he was on this earth. (He couldn't wait till he was seventy-four.)

Heaven.

One year, the last year, she arranged to have another on-again, off-again girlfriend of EB's, Maggie Molloy, sit on the other side of him in the darkened movie house and he took turns kissing them both.

Nirvana.

Just a few weeks after that fourteenth birthday, EB again found himself sitting next to Jenny in the darkened Farragut Movie. It was Saturday afternoon, so of course they were both at the movies. That was the ritual. They were all there. All the kids of EB's neighborhood who could scare up twenty-five cents went to the movies every Saturday. They owned the Farragut Movie on Saturday afternoons.

Jenny had reached puberty a year or so earlier and was showing beautiful signs of becoming a woman. In other words, she had very pretty, newly-budded breasts.

EB and Jenny were "on" at this point and they were kissing. Not making out heavily, but playfully kissing. A peck on the cheek here and there, a brush on the lips every once in awhile. The year was 1948...the very essence of innocence. But Jenny was feeling a little frisky this day.

Fortunately for EB...he was right there, next to her.

Unfortunately for EB...his cousin Barbara was sitting next to him. Sister Mary Barbara they called her.

Jenny snatched EB's baseball hat from his lap, neatly folded it as she had seen him do many times...and put it down the front of her loose-fitting white sailor's blouse. Then she whispered in his ear that she had nothing on underneath and dared him to reach up her blouse and get his hat.

My God...Jesus.

He couldn't breathe; his body was transformed...his mouth was filled with heated cotton balls. He couldn't speak, his heart was exploding...it was coming out of him...it was beating on the seat in front of him...and the kid in that seat could hear it and feel it and was turning around and staring. His eyes weren't working, all he could see were circles...concentric circles...beautiful circles within circles. His hands were shaking and starting to move toward the bottom hem of her blouse of their own accord...out of their own frenzied anticipation.

Jenny, aware of all of this, was smiling an "I'm Eve, you're Adam" smile.

Barbara, aware of all this, was whispering a scream at him...EB, DON'T YOU DARE DO THIS...DON'T YOU DARE PUT YOUR HAND THERE...THAT'S A SIN...THAT'S A MORTAL SIN...YOU'LL GO TO HELL...YOU'LL GO RIGHT PAST PURGATORY DIRECTLY TO HELL...I'LL TELL MY MOTHER...I'LL TELL YOUR MOTHER...I WILL...I'LL TELL MONSIGNOR GEARY...I WILL...I MEAN IT...EB, regaining a measure of composure, now wanted to kill Barbara.

But that was a mortal sin, too.

But why, God? Why did she have to be here? Why now? Why on this day?

This was right out of a movie. He had been dreaming of this for years. No, the truth was, he had not dared to dream of this. This was what all fourteen year old kids dared not dream of (at least in the '40s and '50s in EB's Brooklyn).

But he could make this dream real, make it happen. All he had to do was let his hands do what they wanted to do. Then it would be their fault, not his. He'd be sending his hands to hell, but it would be worth it.

Jenny was smiling and whispering in his ear:
DO IT...GET IT...I WANT YOU TO GET IT.

And Barbara was still quietly screaming into his other ear...I'LL TELL THE BISHOP...I'LL TELL THE CARDINAL...I'LL TELL THE POPE...I'LL NEVER TALK TO YOU AGAIN.

In the end, that last threat was the clincher. He did love his cousin, she was like his older sister. He couldn't lose her respect.

So Jenny retrieved his hat from under her blouse, everything simmered down, and everyone was left with his or her own thoughts.

EB thought about the concept of respect. Maybe he didn't lose Barbara's respect, but did he gain it? Did she respect him any more for this act of heroic Catholic resistance to the Devil's own temptation? (The Devil always took the form of a beautiful girl in the '40s.)

He wasn't sure how lasting that would be.

And what of Jenny? Did she respect what he did? Or better yet, didn't do? Somehow he doubted it.

After this summer, she started to date older guys (seventeen and eighteen), and then she seemed so much older and more sophisticated than EB and his friends. And in her presence they felt more like kids.

That was the end of that puppy love affair.

And what of EB himself?

Enhanced self-respect? Is that what he felt? Partially.

He also felt like a wimp.

Contradictions. Life was full of contradictions.

Is that how a wiseguy should handle the situation?

Naaaahh!

He understood that even though this was relatively innocent and Jenny was as much an old friend as a "girl friend", it was still a kind of grown-up situation.

And he didn't handle it confidently.

In the end, he thought he did the right thing, but yet, he did what Barbara wanted, not what he wanted.

He was still young, he knew that. And not ready.

But he would be next time.

He hoped.

For EB, the summer of 1948 set the pattern for his teenage love life. The coming years would consist of many intermittent two-week love affairs. They would begin with an honest passion and end with a kind of disingenuous lack of emotional commitment on EB's part.

Arrogance.

Dating in the summer also brought another complication. Beautiful summer evenings brought the people of the block out of their homes and onto the stoops.

That meant running the gauntlet.

OHHH, BIG DATE TONIGHT?...WHO'S THE LUCKY GIRL?...DON'T BE HOME TOO LATE...WHAT A HANDSOME BOY...YOU'RE MUCH TOO GOOD FOR HER, EB...DON'T DO ANYTHING WE WOULDN'T DO.

His neighbors would actually shout it out as he passed. It was all in fun, but there was no escape. They knew when he was and when he wasn't dating. When EB was out on a date, he looked different. He wore freshly-creased slacks and a carefully-selected, crisply-ironed shirt (thanks Mom) and his gleaming Flagg Brothers brogues. And this was the year he began shaving. So inevitably he had a cut upper lip and perhaps small pieces of toilet paper still clinging to his jaw, temporarily stemming the blood flow from decapitated pimples.

He was conspicuous as hell.

And there was no hiding. No car to sneak away in.

The gauntlet had to be run.

PROMISE HER ANYTHING, BUT KEEP YOUR FINGERS CROSSED, HAR, HAR (a man)...HEY, EB, I'M FREE TONIGHT (a woman)...WANNA BORROW THE CAR?...WE'LL WAIT UP FOR YA.

He hated it. But he loved it, too.

The year before, EB got his first "season locker" at the Farragut Pool. It cost about eighteen dollars, which doesn't sound like very much now but then it was quite a stretch for his parents. He appreciated the effort his mom and dad made to allow him to join his friends at the Pool.

(As Eddie Mitchell would say later, "Anything for the prince.")

He suspected, though it was never confirmed, that his little sister Dorothy had helped him by offering to make some financial sacrifices to enable their parents to afford this new and unexpected expense.

It was definitely something Dorothy would do.

That summer at the Farragut Pool, EB's friends coalesced into a soft-edged group of ten to fourteen kids (six to eight boys and four to six girls) who hung out together during the summer, stayed together during the winter, and through the years to come. For EB, it was the beginning of some very important life-long friendships.

The Farragut Pool was located on Albany Avenue (East 41st Street) between Glenwood Road and Farragut Road. It was right around the corner from EB's house and had been there for as long as he could remember. It was a large pool, what we would now call Olympic-sized. As you entered the front gate you looked down the length of the pool. In the foreground was the shallow end, one foot of water that gradually deepened to eight feet at the other end. At the deep end of the pool stood two low diving boards, one on each side. On the left, maybe twenty yards in from the side of the pool, was the ping-pong house, and beyond that, deeper on the left, were the "sand beach" and the handball and basketball courts. Straight ahead behind the diving boards stood the men's and women's locker rooms.

On the right was a forty-foot-high water slide. It had wooden steps leading up to it with steel-tubing hand rails. The slide itself was wooden, too, bottom-lined with light-weight steel with sputtering water running down its entire course.

During the summer season, outside the pool on the side-walks of Albany Avenue, passersby would see many a terror-crazed kid escorted down its steep, fearsome steps by a lifeguard.

That height was not the place for the faint of heart.

EB and Matty, of course, loved the water slide.

They descended it in as many ways as you could imagine, except standing, which was strictly prohibited (they were tempted). They'd come down on their stomachs, on their backs, and (pushing it) on their knees. If they came down on their back-sides (the expected way), they would turn it into an unexpected dive in the fraction of a second they had before hitting the water.

Just testing the system.

At this point in his young life, EB was always broke. Flat broke, with no pocket money to speak of. And pocket money was critical to appease his highly-advanced addiction for junk food. A little money was necessary for evening double-scoop ice cream cones, Cokes, or half-pints of hand-packed Borden's Ice Cream at Pease's candy store. As always, he was resourceful. He mooched quarters from the older guys; he "borrowed" from his peers; he returned empty soda bottles; he did chores and took on special jobs for neighbors and local store owners. Occasionally he would pick up a few quarters at the Farragut Pool on his reputation alone. He was always bemused by how the word spread, but sometimes nine or ten year old kids who were there just for the day would approach him with exaggerated shyness, confirm his identity, and ask him to "do the dive". EB would escort them to the one-foot water, agree to dive into it for a quarter per kid. (Yes, it was a sordid way to make money, but anything for a half-pint of Borden's.) EB would take a diver's stance on the side of pool, take a long a pause for effect, sigh deeply, and spring out in a powerful, extremely shallow "racing" dive. He barely penetrated the water, he almost never felt the one-foot bottom of the pool, even with his hands. He simply skimmed along the surface.

Very impressive. The audience always reacted with open-mouthed awe.

It looked a lot more dangerous than it really was, but it did take plenty of technique and he had practiced it for a year. As he walked (sauntered?) away, he always warned the kids not to try it themselves. He owed them that. He owed them a full quarter's worth.

But those opportunities didn't happen often enough and his financial condition was mostly "red" (emergency).

EB loved to sing, and some of his friends told him he did it well. His favorite singer at that time was Perry Como. His friends told EB he sounded just like Mr. Como. He wanted to believe that, but he never did completely. Not completely.

He and Jerry Frost were hanging out in the Farragut Pool on this particular soft and warm summer evening. EB was suffering through a bad case of the cravings for a half-pint of hand-packed Borden's chocolate and peach ice cream. Jerry was always a very generous kid who was doing more than his share of supporting EB through this economically depressed time, and EB didn't want to hit on him for more money.

So he hit on him in another way.

Right there and then, he gave Jerry Frost a battlefield commission. He named him his principle talent agent, (Buddy Bohan, his long-standing agent, didn't have a season locker, and besides, he had been slacking off lately. He wasn't fired, he was simply relegated to sports.) EB asked Jerry if he could convince Margarita Mullins (one of the girls in the group) if she would be willing to pay fifty cents for a little song. Jerry, never one to miss the smile in any situation, agreed to give it a try. And off he went.

And soon returned with Margarita in tow.

EB...eyes twinkling to beat the band...sat her down on a bench fronting the ping-pong house, stood in front of her holding an imaginary microphone, looked directly into her eyes, and crooned "Dreamer's Holiday".

It might have been a little tentative, but EB thought it sounded pretty damn good. To him, objectively, it was a hit.

Perry Como.

At the finish, Jerry (beaming) held out his hand for the fifty cents. Margarita hesitated.

EB panicked; it looked for second there like she wasn't going to pay. But finally she did. And as she passed over the money to Jerry, she looked up at him and with all sincerity said...I DIDN'T THINK IT WAS WORTH IT...and she left.

WHAT A BLOW!...WHAT A BITCH!...said Jerry...WHO DOES SHE THINK SHE IS ANYWAY?...MARTIN BLOCK?... DON'T WORRY ABOUT IT, EB...LET'S GO TO PEASE'S AND GET SOME ICE CREAM...IT'S ON HER, THAT BITCH...

But EB being EB, did worry about it. And he did think about it. Often. Yes, she was only one person (one of those mysterious girl-people to boot), but if he was really as good a singer as some of his friends said he was, she would surely have reacted differently. Margarita was basically a nice person who spoke the truth. A little too directly perhaps, but the truth nevertheless. And maybe his friends were telling him what he wanted to hear, which was quite nice, quite loyal, but not quite the truth.

He loved to sing, he loved to fantasize about it as his future. (Sinatra would see him as his chief rival...and fear him. SINATRA FEARS EB!!! blares the 72-point headline in Variety.) So he questioned it as objectively as he possibly could. Did he have it? He was a pretty good singer, could he be a great singer?

Honestly, he didn't think so.

So maybe he wasn't the second coming of Perry Como after all, but once again, EB learned a valuable lesson. At that point in time he wouldn't have phrased it quite this way, but later on he articulated the lesson like this:

He whom the gods would curse, they would first seem to bless...by bestowing upon him a plenitude of uncommon talent.

But not quite enough.

10 Chapter Ten-Spring

Baseball started in mid-April.

And in EB's opinion, that was about a month too early. Baseball is a summer game, not a winter game. And regardless of what the calendar said, EB insisted that not only was April a winter month, but it was the coldest month of the winter, period! (There was no reasoning with him on this subject.)

Batting practice was brutal. Anything but perfect contact with the ball stung the hands like crazy. It really hurt, but the anticipation was almost worse than the actuality. It got into your head, and your head shouted warnings to your hands and wouldn't shut up and your hands listened. And that could screw up your swing. And one more thing...there were no such things as batting gloves in the '40s and '50s.

If there were, the first kid who tried to wear them would

have been laughed off the field.

Unmanly. Un-Brooklynly.

Would Duke Snider wear a batting glove? Would Jackie Robinson? Would Carl Furillo? (Especially Carl Furillo.) No! Never.

So in April on Kings Field in Brooklyn in the '40s and '50s, you would see kids wince as they began the swing...dreading the pain of contact. Some of the borderline kids on the team prayed for a swing and a miss. In fact, they probably missed on purpose, which is why they were, and always would be, borderline kids. Fielding practice was not all that pleasant, either. But you did it. You showed up after school and on Saturdays and worked out for hours in the cold, cruel, biting winds of April because you were committed to the team and the game.

Then the weather warmed and all of that was forgotten.

Play ball.

Marbles also started in late April. Three games are worthy of note. They had no names, but every kid knew them and played them with a serious mien and a practiced skill.

One popular marble game was played on the dirt. A circle was drawn with a pen knife blade and each player (maximum of four) scattered an agreed-upon number of marbles inside the circle. The object was to knock as many marbles as you could out of the circle, shot by shot. Every marble you knocked out you kept. If you failed to do that on a given shot, you lost your turn and the next shooter took over. Of course there were games within the game; head games were played, strategies were conceived and executed, kibitzing was expected and accepted. For example, when an opponent had a chip shot that could not be missed, someone called, "Rounds, no dubs, knucks down." Translated that meant that the shooter had to move his shot location one hundred eighty degrees around the circle so the shot then had to cover a much greater distance; he could not exchange his marble for his most favorite "shooter" marble, and finally, he must put all four knuckles in the dirt and leave them there, effectively forcing him to shoot with his hand in a contorted, uncomfortable position. As a consequence of this call, a shot that couldn't be missed became a shot that probably shouldn't be taken.

Strategy.

Thinking.

Another marble game was a classic city adaptation. It was played in the street along the curb...and along the curb...and along the curb. It could and sometimes did, last for miles. Lost in concentration for an hour, you could suddenly look up and discover you were in some other neighborhood.

The rules were simple: the first kid shoots (throws) his marble out along the curbside as far as he can, or as close as he dares. The second kid tries to hit it. If he does, he wins that marble and collects any side-bets that were agreed upon in advance (usually paid in "purees"...the best, absolutely certified virginal, and most beautifully colored marbles you possessed). The direction of this game was always straight ahead, you could not shoot backwards, or sideways.

What seemed simple, however, proved to be a lot more complex. "Hits" were not easy to come by. As always, there were strategies, moves and counter moves, arcane rules, and natural forces that added sophisticated levels to the basic form. When you were about to shoot at another kid's marble, he could call "placeees" and replace his normal sized marble with a "pigmy" (which you couldn't hit with a laser). You, on the other hand, could replace your shooting marble with a "kabola" (a giant orb twice the diameter of a regular marble that hit anything and everything in its path).

Strategy.

Thinking.

Any shot had to be carefully considered. Distance and terrain were the determining factors. A successful shot was hardly ever a sure thing, so a miss had to be calculated. You could miss close if you missed short, but if you missed on the long side, it had to be very long or you risked setting up your opponent with a good shot. Another complication was the playing field itself. The street.

It had stuff in it. On it. Over it.

Urban detritus.

Dirt. Bits of gravel, little stones, sticks, rocks, leaves, organic materials.

Stuff.

The streets of Brooklyn were giant receptacles for "stuff", and you were shooting into it, over it, or under it. So you had to factor the vagaries of the terrain into your thinking. For instance, if your opponent's marble was lying just short of a little collection of leaves and twigs, then you could afford to be aggressive because, if you missed just a little bit long, you were protected by the "stuff". Of course, on your adversary's next shot he could call "cleanseees" (to enable him to sweep away the stuff between his marble and yours).

He could call it, but you could disallow it.

Those were the rules. Fashioned over the eons by wise counsels of kid legislators.

You had to love it.

And EB did.

In the spring, he played this game everyday on the way home from school.

Some days it took him three hours to get home.

There was one more marble game that should be noted here. It, too, was a Brooklyn classic. The city equivalent of selling snake oil from the back of a wagon. The quintessential urban scam.

During the spring, older, more accomplished wiseguy-con-artists would appear in the neighborhood. They would place their custom-tailored cardboard shoe boxes against the curb and invite the little kids to step up...TAKE A CHANCE...TEST YOUR SKILL...WIN PRIZES...WIN! WIN! WIN!..And the little kids did take a chance. But, of course, they had no chance at all. The odds here were worse than in Las Vegas.

They stood out in the street, five feet or so from the shoe boxes. The boxes had holes cut into them, four to a box. The size of the holes varied from just a tiny bit wider and taller than a marble to twice that size, with two graduations in between. The little kids rolled their marbles down the convex curve of the street to the boxes trying to enter one of those inviting black holes.

The older wiseguys paid off a successful roll into the different-sized holes with varying-sized, super-attractive payoffs.

But not very often.

When these enterprising future moguls (or politicans) left the neighborhood, they took a good portion of the kids' marble supply with them.

EB and his friends did not admire this genre of wiseguy and stayed away from their games...recognizing a losing proposition when they saw one.

Spring was also the start of a new season of stickball.

Here, too, there were two fundamental forms. The first was the famous one-bounce street game played five to eight kids to a side with the legendary spaldeen for a ball, an old broomstick for a bat, and the natural features of the block for bases. For this game, the baseball diamond shape was slightly distorted and elongated. Home plate was a sewer cover in the center of the street; first base could be the front fender of a parked car; third base the trunk of an old tree. Second base was the next sewer cover. That put second base about one hundred and twenty feet from home (even Roy Campanella would have had a tough time with that). But since there was no stealing, and not a lot of kids were ever thrown out on the bases, it all worked pretty well. This was primarily a game of hitting.

Offense was king.

Defense was death-defying.

A well-hit spaldeen approached a third baseman like a knuckle ball traveling at approximately seven hundred miles an hour. It could rise two feet and go over a kid's head, or it could drop two feet and hit him in the family jewels. Or, it could go straight and hit him between the eyes. What would it do? He had a tiny fraction of a second to figure it out.

No, stickball was not a game of defense.

But offense was a joy beyond description.

The pitcher threw to the hitter on one bounce. There were no balls and strikes, so he waited for the pitch he liked, timed it with two or three strides and whaled away. Off that humble broomstick bat, that big, pink, beautiful spaldeen exploded like a Cape Canaveral space launch.

UP, UP AND AWAY!...SON OF A BITCH!...LOOK AT ME, LOOK!...I AM ABSOLUTELY RUTHIAN!...WHERE ARE THE SCOUTS...YES, I'LL SIGN A CONTRACT!...PAY ME THE MINIMUM...NO, MONEY DOESN'T MATTER...IT'S THE LOVE OF THE GAME...CAN I HIT THE CURVEBALL?...I CRUSH CURVEBALLS!..I CRUSH EVERTHING!!! SIXTY FIVE HOMERS THE FIRST YEAR... GUARANTEED.

Absolutely no argument, hitting a spaldeen was one of the top three things you could do in life.

EB maintains to this day that he was a two and a half sewer man. That would mean that he hit a spaldeen over three hundred feet.

(Suffice it to say that EB's two and a half sewer claim is highly disputed in some quarters.)

Their second version of stickball was, in some ways, the mirror image of the first. A pitcher's game. A game of finesse.

It was primarily a one-on-one game in which the pitcher threw to a batter who stood in front of a wall. On the wall was a vertical rectangular box outlined in white paint that represented the strike zone of some long ago forgotten kid who fit its dimensions. With the passing years it had become a generic strike zone. It fit everyone. Or, more to the point, everyone had to fit it. Tall or short, this was your strike zone. Live with it. The particular paint-box strike zone in EB's life was on the brick wall of PS 198, the public grammar school located on the corner of Albany Avenue and Farragut Road opposite Paerdegat Park.

In the spring, EB played "fast pitch" stickball games every day of the week after school. They were nine-inning games, but the batter only got one out, so the games tended to be fast-paced and short. That meant he could play two or three nine inning games a day.

The pitcher stood on a chalk-marked "pitching rubber" (actually, by that time, a well-worn indentation in the cement surface of the schoolyard). It was a carefully measured sixty feet six inches from the plate (a yellow painted square with a pointed side that exactly replicated a major league home plate). It was precisely the width of the strike zone box painted on the wall.

All very official.

Of course, "fast pitch" was played with the sainted pink spaldeen and the requisite broomstick bat. The pitcher could use all the weapons at his command; fastballs, curves, drops, risers, changes of pace, spitballs. Everything was legal. The batter swung at everything he liked. If he took a pitch that was inside the box or on the line, it was a strike. Outside the line was a ball. Four balls was a walk; three strikes, you're out! One out per inning. Anything hit past the pitcher on the ground was a single.

Anything on the ground that the pitcher could reach had to be fielded cleanly to be an out. If the pitcher bobbled it at all, it was a single.

Parallel to the wall, out about a hundred yards and running the entire width of the schoolyard, was a two-tiered chain-link fence. Any ball hit off the bottom tier on the fly was a double; off the top tier was a triple; over the fence was a home run. Foul poles were clearly marked left and right.

Those were the rules. Strictly enforced. Universally obeyed.

Yes, the code.

EB considered this game a gift from the gods and played it as often as possible. He played against every kid he knew older kids, peers, and younger kids, anyone who was willing. He played it well, winning his share of games and losing his share of games, too. They all played it well.

He and Buddy Bohan organized a league (Bohan was commissioner, of course) consisting of a half dozen kids from 40th Street. They chipped in a few dollars apiece (losing their amateur status), created schedules, and kept stats. Suddenly, winning and losing became a serious business.

Professionals.

Every spring and running into the summer, stickball was played in schoolyards all over Brooklyn. Skillful, intense competition that honed the body, sharpened the mind, and defined the time.

The Golden Age.

Looking back and reflecting on that time of fast-pitch stickball, EB would tell you (with his well-developed gift for understatement) that he pitched more nine inning-games than Cy Young.

Spring was also a time for goin' fishin'.

But Brooklyn fishing was a totally different concept than Kansas City fishing. EB and his friends would take the Flatbush Avenue trolley car to the end of the line at Avenue U. They would then walk the two and a half miles to the Brooklyn side of the Marine Park bridge. On the way, they would stop at a bait shop and buy a cardboard container of blood worms.

Beneath the bridge were old dilapidated piers and long-neglected, rotted pilings stretching out into Jamaica Bay. The kids would walk twenty-five feet or so out to the end of these little piers (nobody else would trust the integrity of those structures, but EB and the rest of the kids knew them well) and rig their lines. Which meant they would attach the worms to their little hooks, tie on the sinkers, unwind fifty feet of line from its spool, secure the spool end to a piling, whirl the line around their heads, and fling it out into the water.

And go off to play Ring-o-livio.

(Brooklyn fishing was an exquisite and unique art form.)

After an hour or so, they would return and reel in their fish. The catches were mainly sea robins or an occasional flounder. Hardly game fish, but since this area of Jamaica Bay was considered polluted, it didn't much matter; you couldn't eat them anyway.

One Saturday in mid-spring of 1949, EB and his cousin Matty were "Brooklyn fishing" under the Marine Park bridge with a rather unusual cast of characters. Ed Stuchbury (one of the Farragut Pool group) was there that day, so was Dick Duckett. And so were the manic Rae brothers, Stevie and Peter.

Dick Duckett was another of the neighborhood's demi-gods. But Dick was more than that; to EB (little romantic that he was), Dick was the whole Pantheon. The god of gods. In a neighborhood of very good ballplayers, Duckett was the best. Name the sport...he was great. Basketball?...he made the NBA (a cup of coffee in the late fifties with the Cincinnati Royals...you could look it up). Baseball?...he was great. Softball?...he pitched and hit fourth. Football?...the quarterback. Swimming?...he beat you. Riding waves?...he was up at the boardwalk.

Every game they played, Duckett played it better than anybody.

Board games? Checkers? Chess? Monopoly? Parcheesi? He beat you.

Life? That was his best game.

And that was his secret...his strength and his weakness. Every aspect of his life was a game. He approached the act of ordering a hamburger at the local diner with the same conceptual intensity as he did winning a championship basketball game for

St. John's University.

He was cool and calculating...he was manic and impatient. He was devoted, dedicated, and disciplined...he was careless, aloof, and disinterested. He was kind and giving most of the time, and cruel and bullying some of the time. He was imaginative, flamboyant, unpredictable, explosive, and always the leader.

Duckett taught EB how to play basketball. Introduced him to the nuances and subtleties of the inner game...the game within the game. Earlier, when EB was twelve (Duckett was almost three years older), Dick practically adopted him. Beyond his tutoring, on Saturday mornings in Paerdegat Park he would pick EB to be on his team in serious, three-man, half-court blood games with the older guys. Then it would be EB, Jack Prenderville, and Duckett against the oldest, biggest, and baddest guys in the neighborhood. EB knew he had no business being in those games, but Dick had a subtle sense of singularity and thought he could get away with anything. And the fact that he would try to get away with almost everything endeared him to EB even more.

Dick Duckett was well aware of how much the younger kids looked up to him. He reveled in it, he thrived on it, but he also understood the responsibilities that went with it. He handled that part well.

To sum it up, to EB and to most of the other kids in the neighborhood, Dick Duckett was a hero.

He was also a little nuts.

As were the Rae brothers.

Stevie was the oldest, about Duckett's age. He had straight black hair, he was tall and lean and loud...full of energy. Manic. Always talking, moving, waving his arms and his legs like the Scarecrow in the Wizard of Oz. EB loved to be on his side when they played "guns" because Stevie had a wonderful repertoire of great sound effects. He kept up a constant cacophony of incoming and outgoing exploding, whizzing, ricocheting bullets that lent a kind of weird reality to the game. You would always find EB by his side when they played "guns". Peter was two years younger. He had tight, curly red hair. (Don't think that didn't cause some talk around neighborhood.) Physically, except for the hair, they were very much alike...Peter was just as big and just as manic as Stevie, but in a different way.

Steve was harmless; Peter was not.

There was a dark side to Peter. He lacked the humor of his brother. And the restraint. And Peter was not on line the day God handed out the great gift of subtlety.

EB lived across the street from the Rae brothers so he saw a lot of them. Somehow he often found himself going to the movies with Peter.

He hated that.

If they saw Tyrone Power in the "Black Swan" at the Farragut Movie, Peter would force EB into sword fights all the way home. They always cut through the "woods", and on the way Peter would pull up a couple of four-foot weeds with one-inch stalks, tear off the leaves, toss one to EB, and cry...EN GARDE! Then he'd try to run EB through with his makeshift weed-sword.

Then Peter would run ahead and disappear. Then he'd leap down on EB's back as he passed under a tree limb spanning the dirt trail. (At this point in time Peter was four inches taller and forty pounds heavier than EB.)

Penalty flag! Piling on!

If they saw "Guadulcanal Diary." Peter would insist that EB was a Japanese soldier and try to spin him into the weeds with jujitsu throws. If they saw a John Wayne western, Peter would engage EB in a pretend barroom brawl that got a little too close to real. Peter was a little crazy.

He was also dangerous.

On this day, they had all been under the bridge for most of the day. It was about three in the afternoon and they had just checked their fishing lines for the last time. Normally they simply dumped the fish they caught back into Jamaica Bay. But Duckett was there this day...doing his thing.

Through the day they had caught about a half dozen sea robins and Dick was offended at the thought that these innocent little fish would simply be thrown back into the Bay. The boys had killed them; it was their responsibility to treat those ugly little bodies with respect.

So they were directed to dig six graves and bury them.

Now at three o'clock in the afternoon, the six boys were

standing in a circle on the sands of Jamaica Bay staring down at the bodies of three more very dead sea robins.

They were arguing, as always.

Everybody wanted to go home and forget about this bizarre little ritual. But Dick stood fast. And now upped the ante by insisting that these last three fish of the day be buried with full honors.

Including little crosses on the graves.

With a collective groan, the other five kids gave in to the demi-god. And set to work digging the graves in the hard-packed sand. EB and the Rae brothers dug with the World War II Bowie knives they had recently received from a mail order house. The knives came in a very fancy leather carrying cases but looked like irregular, dull, misshapen, miniature bayonets. But they only cost ninety-nine cents, so what could you expect?

So it was done. The graves were dug, the fish lowered into their eternal resting places and covered with sand. The crosses were in place, fashioned from little pieces of driftwood, the cross pieces secured with fishing line. As Dick recited the benediction, EB, Matty, Stuchbury, and Steve Rae stood in a circle over the graves with bowed heads.

And zany Peter knelt in the sand, head hung in mock gravity while Dick rattled on and on, playing out the scene. A Barrymore, always. Finally, he finished.

And Steve, in a final, exasperated emotional comment, aimed his ninety-nine cent Bowie knife at the graves and flung it down. Just as Peter, still kneeling, thrust out his hand to make a final adjustment to one of the crosses.

The boys let out a collective gasp as the six-inch blade buried itself in the back of Peter's hand.

Silence.

Time stood still. The waves stopped lapping at the shore line. The air around them was suddenly a vacuum. Nothing moved. What would happen now? What would the mercurial Peter do? Would he try to knife his brother? Would they witness a double murder? This was serious. This was Peter Rae.

They waited.

Peter moved only his head; his arm stayed outstretched, supporting that big, dull, cheap knife semi-embedded in the back of his hand.

He looked up at his brother Steve...
The other boys were holding their breaths...
Peter stared up at Steve and said...
YOU PROBABLY THINK THAT HURTS...

EB snuck a look at Duckett; he knew he shouldn't, but he did. Dick's cheeks were starting to billow. He looked like he was ready to explode.

That did it. They all let loose in unison.

Laughter. Hysterics.

The hard, embarrassing truth is EB and those four boys convulsed onto the sand. Holding their sides in pain, they howled for five minutes.

And the ever-unpredictable Peter laughed with them.

When they regained control of themselves, they removed the knife and wrapped Peter's hand in a couple of almost clean handkerchiefs, went up onto Flatbush Avenue and flagged down a passing car to take Peter and Steve to Coney Island Hospital.

The other four boys walked back to Avenue U.

Laughing all the way.

Oh, that Peter, what a funny guy.

11 Chapter Eleven-Fall

Brooklyn was called the borough of churches.

It could have been called the borough of trees.

And at no time of the year was that more appropriate and apparent than in the fall. Millions of trees doing their autumnal thing. Bestowing on the neighborhood their visual, tactile, and olfactory gifts.

The sensual season.

First came the show of sometime intense, sometime subtle, always changing colors for the eye, then the crisp, fallen leaves for the hands and feet and finally the evocative autumn fragrance of burning leaves for the nose. Yes, burning leaves was legal in the '40s and '50s, and the good burghers of Brooklyn raked up and burned piles of leaves to keep them from blowing onto their next door neighbors' lawns. The adults set their fires in the street next to the curb, tended them, kept them small and contained, feeding the fire small piles of leaves after it had consumed the previous ones. They were careful with the leaves.

They were adults.

EB and his friends, on the other hand, were not so careful.

They were kids.

Piles of leaves were irresistible. They were there to dive into, to hide under, to wrestle in, to throw, to scatter, and finally, to burn.

EB and Matty became aware of and quickly adopted an interesting tool they used only in the fall. With it they could set leaves on fire from fifty feet away.

A truly inspired, diabolical, wiseguy invention.

All they needed was one of their mother's empty (or emptied) wooden thread spools, a thick rubber band, and two thumbtacks. And a box of Diamond Blue Tip kitchen matches. That was it. Simple. But diabolical.

The spools were sturdy, inch and a half wooden cylinders with center holes about one-quarter inch in diameter. Viewed from EB's perspective, those holes were like the miniature barrels of a cannon. A three-eights inch wide rubber band was cut to fit around the end of the spool, centered over the end hole, and fastened on each side of the spool with a thumbtack. A wooden kitchen match was fed into the hole, pushed through to the rubber band like an arrow to a bow. Then, the end of the match inside the rubber band was grasped by the index finger and thumb, pulled back, and let go.

Silently, the little wooden arrow with the blue tip was up and on its way. And when it landed, it ignited. If they shot it high, it burst into flame and stayed where it landed. But if they shot it at a shallow angle, they could skip it, burning, into a pile of leaves.

EB and Matty were in agreement that the latter approach was the most interesting. Sometimes they would lie and wait for a likely looking adult "mark", a man preferably, who was walking by and, lost in reverie or deep thought, not paying attention. The boys would hide behind shrubbery or bushes close to the sidewalk and close to a pile of leaves in front of the walker. As the mark approached, the boys would send two match arrows skipping into the pile of leaves. If the timing was perfect, as the man passed the leaves they would suddenly leap into flame.

MY GOD...WHAT THE HELL...(looking around)... NOBODY HERE...WOW, SPONTANEOUS COMBUSTION!...I DON'T BELIEVE IT...NEVER SAW THAT BEFORE...(he easily stomped out the few burning leaves). And stood looking around, looking and not quite believing...SPONTANEOUS COMBUS- TION! WOW!...NO, WAIT A SECOND...C'MON...IT'S TOO COLD FOR THAT, ISN'T IT?...WHAT THE HELL...Most marks didn't get involved in the details, but some of the younger ones did. Most of the older men kind of panicked, and sometimes EB and Matty suddenly appeared and helped put out the fledgling flames, for which they were profusely thanked. But the younger men were unpredictable. When a young guy started looking closer, getting down, examining things, and found the match sticks, then EB and Matty took off behind the bushes into the backyards. And started leaping over fences. Those young guys are the ones who will chase you.

And sometimes they're pretty fast.

One late fall night, EB was walking down Farragut Road with his father. His father was momentarily "on the wagon" so he was himself. And that made EB feel good. And frisky.

He had his "spool" with him on this night. And every once in a while, walking next to his father, he would silently launch a "blue arrow" at a high angle and out to the side. Suddenly in the darkness, there would be a flash of light out on the street that quickly flamed and died. EB's father saw it and stopped. Looked, paused, started walking again. He didn't say anything. Not sure what he saw. EB was silent.

EB loosed another arrow.

Again, twenty five feet to the side, the street flashed and darkened again.

His father kept walking. Without looking at EB he said ...DID YOU DO THAT?...EB didn't say a word. But loosed another match stick.

Again it hit, flamed, and died.

They walked on together.

Without a word, EB's father put out his hand. EB unpalmed his spool and placed it into his father's hand. They stopped...GIVE ME A MATCH STICK...With just a moment's study there on the darkened street, his father loaded the match stick and launched a blue arrow; it arched out into the night sky, crashed into the middle of the street, flamed up and then out.

They resumed their walk.

THIS COULD BE DANGEROUS...ARE YOU BEING CAREFUL...BETTER YET, ARE YOU BEING RESPONSIBLE? ...YES, DAD...(with fingers just a little crossed). The father handed the spool back to the son, and for the first time EB looked up at his father's face.

He was smiling.

EB felt good. Sober dads were the best. To think that some kids had this all the time...well, good for them. He was envious of that, but right there, right then, he felt warm and good.

His father put his arm around EB's shoulder and, still smiling, said to his son...YOU'RE QUITE THE LITTLE WISEGUY, AREN'T YOU?...

Now EB was smiling too.

In Brooklyn, as everywhere else in America, football was the game of the fall season. It started in August, co-existed with roller skating for a month and then owned the rest of the year until its season ended, at least when they were young, in late November. They played in the streets...two-hand touch with as many as six kids to a side and as few as three. The entire width of the street was the field, with the curbs as the side lines. Sewer covers were the goal lines. That meant the field was one hundred twenty feet long and fifty feet wide. They tried to play between sewers where there were no parked cars, but after 1945 that became more and more difficult. So parked cars were sometimes part of the field and part of the offensive and defensive strategies...BOHAN, GO DOWN THE MIDDLE AND CUT TO THE FRONT OF THE BLUE STUDEBAKER....said the designated quarterback of the day...EB, GO DOWN THE MIDDLE AND CUT TO THE BACK OF THE WHITE BUICK, I'M GONNA THROW IT HIGH SO USE THE BUMPER TO CLIMB UP THERE AND GET IT...

Passing was the name of the game. Running plays were usually not that successful. The team on defense had to wait three seconds before it could make a move to rush the passer...ONE MISSISSIPPI...TWO MISSISSIPPI...THREE MISSIS-

SIPPI...so the passer had plenty of time to scan the field. There was no blocking. Two hands anywhere on the man with the ball meant he was "down". There were first downs at the usual ten yard intervals. They were marked with anything the kids could find...school bags, soda bottles, newspapers, somebody's hat, or the bodies of kids waiting to play the "winner".

Rough tackle was played in the woods on the field they called the Plateau. It was a brutal surface, uneven, hard, rutted, eroded. Dangerous for ankles and knees. The equipment they wore was not much help, either. Old, hand-me-down shoulder guards and helmets that were worn out, out-of-date, and probably just as potentially injurious to the kids as the field was. These games were usually played with a full complement of eleven kids per side. They were usually challenges...block against block, class against class. So they were serious games, competitive games, and kids got hurt.

EB played in these games but found them formless and graceless, amateurish and dangerous. And as he grew older, he spent more and more of his autumn seasons on the basketball courts of Paerdegat Park.

So those were the seasons.

The seasons that, one by one, finally added up to the highly textured years of EB and his friends, and all the Brooklyn kids who lived through the Golden Age. Each season had an identity, a personality different from the others. Each season had its own feeling, games, rules, sights, sounds, and smells and held the intense interest of the kids for just the right amount of time before it made way for the next.

Each year had a rhythm and they were into it, feeling it.

They created it themselves, the kids did. Adults didn't do it for them. Adults didn't understand it; adults were virtually unaware of it all. The kids created it, shaped it, ordered it, and passed it down, generation to generation, like primal traditions told and retold around forgotten Pleistocene campfires. Each succeeding generation massaged it a little, improving it here, tightening it there, but never changing the basic idea. They created a life that was always changing, always challenging, but always predictable because it had rules.

And they made the rules.

12

If St. Vincent Ferrer was the official religious and cultural center of EB's neighborhood, then Pease's candy store was the unofficial learning center.

It was where you learned all the necessary social skills.

You learned how to spit.

You learned how to curse.

You learned how to smoke.

You learned to respect your elders (older kids).

You learned how to debate.

You learned how to get along while staying strong.

You learned about life.

Everybody was there. Everybody was always there. EB was always there. For as long as he could remember, he was there. When he was very young, he loved to sit in the back where the pot-bellied stove and tables and chairs were and listen to the older guys in their endless ball-busting, tongue-in-cheek debates.

Just listen, like a seminarian in a monastery. And the older guys allowed that because they were always acutely aware of their responsibilities as role models and teachers of the not yet fully formed.

EB remembered one such debate where his cousin John Campbell was holding court against the rest of the room. It seemed that John's position was not widely held. In fact, he was a majority of one (no surprise there). There were at least six of John's peers arguing with him and sometimes screaming at his intransigence.

His position on that particular day was that we, or he, did not need the sun to live.

He held his own for a half hour or so, but they were chipping away at him. Health, vitamin D, absence of warmth, the presence of numbing cold, encroaching glaciers, too little of the life-giving light, too much of the killing dark, the dying environment, the lack of trees, lumber, water, graze for animals were all the good arguments they used against him. He was getting weaker, but when they used the ultimate weapon of food...growing food in a world without a sun...it looked like he was finished. He bought some time by getting his protagonists to agree that the sun would likely disappear gradually, not cataclysmically. He was thinking fast, but the end was near.

Now they had him in a completely darkened, freezing cold world; nothing grew, nothing breathed, nothing moved.

Finis.

What do you do now, John? They all leaned in, expecting capitulation. John leaned back (smugly, sorry to say) and announced that now he would take off in his rocket ship.

What rocket ship was that?

The rocket ship he built while the sun was gradually going dark. The rocket ship he built while they were all standing around wringing their hands. The rocket ship bound for the constellation Virgo where there was plenty of sun.

Stunned silence.

(To EB, John was brilliant. A little deranged, but brilliant.)

Briefly, they remained silent. They were not expecting this and had to regain their equilibrium. The truth was, John cheated a little (or a lot) by refocusing the argument and moving it into interplanetary travel. They didn't mind that; their code allowed creative cheating so they expected something. But not an inspired escape to Virgo. That surprised them.

Now they needed a killer rejoinder.

Suddenly, the legendary Skippy Devoy leaned into John's face and reminded him that they had agreed that the sun had been gradually darkening for many years and had been completely dark for some time. So there was no food! Nothing had grown for years and years. What would he eat on his rocket ship journey to the constellation Virgo?

The question hung in the air.

They had him this time.

John Campbell calmly took a couple of beats, looked Skippy right in the legendary eye, and calmly announced...I WOULD EAT LIKE A KING...BECAUSE EARLY IN THE CONSTRUCTION I STOCKED MY ROCKET SHIP WITH FIVE HUNDRED THOUSAND FROZEN BALONEY SANDWICHES...

Brilliant.

The back of Pease's candy store erupted in gales of laughter, guys were falling on the floor, holding their sides.

EB was very proud of his older cousin.

Pease's candy store was on the north side of Glenwood Road, the third of three identical storefronts off the corner of Albany Avenue. The unit on the corner was McDade's Saloon. The second from the corner was Joe's Barber Shop. The third was Pease's. The other side of the street was the virtual mirror image. On the corner was Dubin's Drug Store, next was the Ideal Meat Market, next was Vick's Grocery, next Wenn's Deli, and last in line was Gray's Real Estate, later to become a liquor store.

Booze, beer, companionship, cigarettes, egg creams, ham sandwiches, pain relievers, and a shave and a haircut...what more could you ask? A man could live his entire life on that corner.

And some men damn near did.

The interior of Pease's was a dark, elongated rectangle. As you entered, on your left was the requisite cigar/cigarette counter, on your right were the comic book and magazine stands. Further in on the left, the soda fountain began and ran about twenty feet to the back tables and the previously mentioned pot-bellied stove. On the right ran the penny and five-cent candy counters. There were no windows except the big window that spanned the front entrance. But there was a skylight over the back tables - the only natural light source in the interior space. It didn't help that there was a dearth of color. Lots of browns. Brown counters, brown moldings, beige walls.

It doesn't sound like it, but it was a happy place. And EB spent a good part of his early life there. When he was twelve he got a Brooklyn Eagle newspaper route (East 39th Street from Cortelyou Road to Foster Avenue). He kept it for a year, and for the first time in his life he had pocket money. (Discretionary spending, what a great concept.) After "doing his route" in those days, he would ride his hand-me-down bike to Pease's to gab, sip a soda, or suck on an ice cream cone. Sometimes, in the spring, he'd buy a half-pint of Borden's ice cream, hand-packed by an older teenager that he knew well, so it was generously over-filled (most times the height of the overflow was almost equal to the height of the cardboard carton itself), and take that bulging container home to eat while listening to the Brooklyn Dodger game on the radio. He had a weakness for ice cream. As well as the Dodgers. But on most days, he just hung around Pease's, inside or outside depending on the time of year and the weather, talking, listening, philosophizing, debating, forming friendships, cementing relationships, learning, evolving.

Mr. Malcolm Pease was a benevolent dictator. He was a nice man who truly liked and enjoyed the kids, but he, like anyone else, had his limits. He would clear the place out on a whim (or more likely a realization that his store was very crowded but he was not making very much money)...AWWRIGHT!...EVERYBODY OUT...DON'T YOU KIDS HAVE HOMES?...GO SEE YOUR MOTHER...GIVE HER A KISS FOR ME...TELL YOUR FATHER I SAID HELLO...OUT!...EVERBODY OUT!...Fifteen or twenty kids would dutifully spill out of Pease's candy store onto the sidewalk and congregate in small groups, talking and waiting. When they figured enough time had gone by and Mr. Pease had returned to his senses and was starting to feel lonely, they'd quietly move back into the store, one by one, two by two. The trick here was to buy something...an egg cream or a cherry Coke would do it. Mr. Pease was doing some business, so he was happy again. Pretty soon the place was just as crowded as before. And the planet was back in its proper orbit.

There were, however, more serious sanctions for more serious transgressions. You could be banished for certain sins. Mr. Pease was sole judge and jury in such instances. He could and would "86" you for any length of time as he saw fit. And he kept track of the days. You could not sneak back in before you served your time in Siberia. He also employed older teenage kids who had the power to punish. Most of them used it sparingly. A few didn't.

For a while one summer, a kid named McAllister worked behind the counter in Pease's. He was older (maybe seventeen), tall (six foot two) and slim, and very imperious. A bit of a pain in the ass. One day when Mr. Pease was absent, he verbally abused the thirteen-year-old EB and his cousin Matty for some damn reason they did not even understand. But the more they protested, the more he poured on the verbal abuse. He browbeat them pretty good. And he wanted them out...out!

So they left.

And waited for him to finish his shift. When he emerged from the store, EB and Matty went after him. They got him on the front lawn of the house next door to Pease's. After some back and forth verbal posturing, EB and Matty jumped him.

Together.

They beat him up pretty good.

(Now it should be noted that this was not very bloody fighting. The code said you did not punch someone you knew, someone in the neighborhood, with your fists, at least not in the face. Punching in the stomach was permissible. But this fighting was about wrestling. A lot of rolling around in the dirt, grappling for holds, and working for the finality of the headlock. A good headlock was the final bell. When you got caught in a headlock, you had two choices: you could "cry uncle" or you could get your brains squeezed out. When you did the smart thing and gave up, the fight was over. The participants of these fights got some cuts and scratches at the most. Pants and shirts took a physical beating, but it was the self-esteem of the loser that suffered the most damage.)

EB and Matty together subdued McAllister pretty quickly.

He sulked his way home and they went around the corner to the Farrgut Pool to symbolically wash away their sins.

They knew it was not over. They knew they were in trouble. There was a multitude of witnesses, so they couldn't say it was his word against theirs.

Or claim a case of mistaken identity.

Nailed.

So they waited for Malcolm Pease's justice.

And it didn't take long. The next day when they showed up at the candy store, they didn't go inside right away because they thought that a casual approach of trying to ease their way back into polite candy store society might work. But word spread quickly. And before they had a chance to go to Mr. Pease, he came out to them.

HE WAS ASHAMED OF THEM...FIGHTING WAS A SIN...AND IF THAT WASN'T BAD ENOUGH, THE TWO OF YOU GANGED UP ON THAT ONE POOR BOY...HOW CRUEL...HOW UNFAIR...TWO BULLIES...COMMON STREET URCHINS...I SHOULD TELL YOUR FATHERS, BUT I WON'T...YOU'LL HAVE TO BE PUNISHED...I DON'T WANT YOU IN MY STORE FOR AWHILE...A LONG WHILE...HAVE YOU ANYTHING TO SAY FOR YOURSELVES?...

EB and Matty, heads down, contrite, tried to explain how McAllister went after them for no reason. They said that he was the cruel one and the bully. Mr. Pease listened to all of that but seemed unmoved. He was stuck on the undeniable fact that they had jumped him together. That was bad. Unforgivable. Two against one. How could they do that? Why?

EB and Matty looked up at Mr. Pease and, in all sincerity, explained their actions in the exquisitely logical truth of the streets:

...MR. PEASE, HE'S TWICE AS BIG AS WE ARE...

Well, not quite, Mr. Pease probably thought to himself, but they did have a point. Mr. Pease looked at the two boys, not unkindly, EB thought later, and told them he was banishing them from the premises for a week.

To the other kids on the corner that day, the ruling seemed harsh, but fair. But to EB and Matty, that was nothing. They were happy and relieved. They expected a lifetime ban.

And how could they have lived with that?

102

All the sharp kids hung out at Pease's. And there was a definite hierarchy. At the bottom were the kids under twelve. Then the age groups ascended from there in soft-edged, two-year units, from thirteen/fourteen, through fifteen/sixteen, and finally reached the top with the very worldly seventeen/eighteen and even older guys. After eighteen, most of the self-appointed sophisticates graduated to McDade's Saloon.

EB thought of all of these age groups as "generations". Each generation teaching the succeeding one the ways of the world. In this way the younger kids respected the older kids. And it all hung together.

And they all hung together.

On a Friday evening in the summer, if you passed the corner of Glenwood Road and Albany Avenue, you might think that this was the center of the universe. It was that crowded. It seemed to EB like hundreds of kids were there, but thirty to fifty kids is probably closer to the truth. The whole thing was free-flowing, organic, alive, moving, pausing, stopping, forming, then pulling apart, then re-forming. Covering the sidewalk from Pease's to McDade's. Each group independent within the whole. But still part of the whole. And it all hung together.

And they all hung together.

There was hardly ever any trouble within the sub-culture of the candy store. The trouble usually came from outside. And it never came on a weekday night. Trouble always came on Friday or Saturday night.

There was a little cement ledge that separated the candy store property from the one-family home next door. It ran on a ninety-degree angle from the end of the front window out to the sidewalk. It stood about a foot high. It sat six kids. That's where EB was the night the bad guys appeared out of nowhere.

Suddenly, a dozen eighteen-year old guys materialized out of the night and were standing on the corner, looking mean and holding baseball bats and tire irons. To EB, who was thirteen, those guys looked very old and very big and very tough. And very scary.

The good guys came pouring out of Pease's, but it was eight o'clock on a soft, summer Friday night and a lot of them

103

had already left for their dates. So the ones that were left were woefully outnumbered. The bad guys, from St. Thomas Aquinas parish and led by a well-known tough kid named McClusky, slowly, menacingly, advanced from the corner to the barber shop, semi-surrounding the six to eight Pease guys who were looking a little uncomfortable and trying desperately not to show it.

If they were uncomfortable, EB and his friends, sitting not ten feet away, were absolutely scared shitless. And trying desperately not to show it.

McClusky announced that they wanted Mindy Bassey (who evidently was guilty of some serious trespass on McClusky's turf, probably involving a girl, but EB wasn't really sure). And if they didn't get him, they'd beat up on whoever was handy. Meaning anyone standing (or sitting) on the corner.

They moved closer. The tension was tightening. This was serious shit.

Gulp.

Then the revered Pease elders arrived. The ancients. The gods. They didn't come from the heavens or the whirling mists.

They came from McDade's Saloon.

Ten of them. Maybe twelve. Bob Campbell, Leo Hart, Duke Ready, both Manning brothers, Frank Pedlow, Dick Duckett's older brother Bob...the oldest guys that EB knew from the neighborhood. They were so old they were practically men. Some of them even had jobs. And there they were, filing out of the saloon, silently forming up in back of McClusky's band of would-be raiders.

Saved.

McClusky was now surrounded.

Now there was a new kind of tension. And EB liked this kind better.

What would happen now?

Well, what happened was what usually happened. They talked it over. Led by the wise old elders, they talked it through. Finally, they agreed that Mindy Bassey and a kid appointed by McClusky would fight it out, one-on-one. That agreed upon, the whole crowd walked down Albany Avenue to Farragut Road and Paerdegat Park, through the softball field and basketball courts to the fenced, grassy area on the Foster Avenue side of the park.

That was the designated boxing ring.

The two gladiators then scaled the four-foot fence and prepared to fight. The arena was now encircled by a swollen crowd of about sixty kids representing both sides, but the preponderance of them were obviously rooting for Mindy Bassey.

It was a warm night. The two fighters stripped off their shirts. That was all the preparation that was necessary. Fists were bare, there were no rules except that both agreed to make it a fair fight. One of the Pease elders told them to fight.

And so they did.

The crowd of onlookers was loud and boisterous at the start but that didn't last long. Quickly the crowd quieted and finally grew silent. If you asked EB about that fight today, he would tell you it was the most terrible thing he had ever seen. This no-name kid from St. Thomas Aquinas beat the hell out of Bassey. He wore a school ring on his left hand, and he used a left jab and that ring to shred Mindy Bassey's face.

It was awful. It looked bad. It sounded worse.

THUNK-RIP, THUNK-RIP, THUNK-RIP...every jab got through and did more damage than a roundhouse right. Somebody should have forced him to remove that ring before the fight. But it was too late. Every little jab left a tear in the skin. Bassey lost interest in throwing punches and was now a helluva lot more interested in protecting his face, which began to ooze blood like a slow motion waterfall. Quickly it covered his entire face, obliterating his identity.

It was terrible.

It was over. It wasn't a fight; it was surgery. And the anesthetic was thirty shots to the head.

Finally, one of the older guys jumped the fence and stopped the operation.

The patient didn't die, but it was close.

McClusky and his people had their honor restored, got their pound of flesh (almost literally), so they went back to their neighborhood without much fuss or further bluster. That would have been a violation of the code.

The dispute was resolved.

Each side played its role with a face-saving swagger. So in the years to come when they told and retold the tale, they could both add in a little bragging. Except for Bassey, of course.

For Bassey there was no brag in that night.

And then came 1950.

To EB it was more unexpected, more unbelievable than what was to come at the end of the 1957 baseball season...when the Dodgers left for Los Angeles.

This was worse, much worse, if you can imagine that.

Malcolm Pease sold the candy store.

Malcolm Pease sold the candy store!

Malcolm Pease sold the candy store!

(Extra! Extra! Read all about it!)

A tragedy.

A crime.

The beginning of the end...the end of the beginning.

Shit.

And talk about unexpected...Mr. Pease sold the store to two Jewish men. Andy and Danny, two tiny little Jewish men, now owned Pease's Candy Store, the St. Vincent Ferrer annex.

Amazing.

Could they grant dispensations for Sunday Mass? No! Could they offer plenary indulgences? No! Could they advise on matters of faith and morals? No! Could they debate the doctrine of the Immaculate Conception? No!

What the hell was the world coming to?

And what would EB's friends and neighbors think of it all? Well, the truth is, they didn't like it very much, at least in the beginning. In the beginning, the two Jews were sorely tested. A lot of taunting was tried, a moderate amount of mischief was committed, a bit of anti-Semitism was verbalized, all conceived to get these two guys to reconsider the deal. And fold.

They didn't.

They hung in there, fought back when they felt they should and smiled when they felt they could. Slowly, they become a part of the neighborhood. Andy left after a year or so, but Danny was there for the duration. In time, he became as much of an institution as Mr. Pease ever was.

And of course he became a good friend to EB and most of the other boys.

So things were changing. The neighborhood was changing. The world was changing.

Especially on the Korean Peninsula.

13

EB's class average for the eight years in St. Vincent Ferrer's was 93/94%. And that simple fact eased his journey through grammar school.

Yes, he was a wiseguy, but he was a smart wiseguy.

The nuns would forgive a lot if they saw that you were actually learning. That meant that they were even getting through to the behaviorally challenged...and that after all, was their vocation.

By definition, a Brooklyn wiseguy had a lively, subtle, inquiring mind. EB paid attention in class, he listened, he was active, he participated, particularly in discussions that interested him. He understood the game.

He was a player.

And that made him a great test taker.

To EB, a test was just another competition. A game. One

on one. Mano a mano, or in this case, boy against nun, kid against institution. He was like a crossword puzzle addict who lives to get into the head of the creator. He looked for tendencies, he listened for emphasis in the classroom, he filed away past tests in his memory bank, he looked for favorite questions, repeats, likes and dislikes. Taking the tests, he laughed at the softballs the nuns threw in for the learning-impaired of the class and was on the lookout for the traps they set for the brainy ones.

Tests were wonderful fun.

Especially the more formal mid-term and final exams.

EB was always the first one in the class to finish. He trusted his instincts. The first answer that came into his head was the right one. He prepared well and he never second-guessed himself. He flew through every test, signed the Catholic school mandatory honesty statement that he had not cheated...I DO SO DECLARE...left his seat, sidled out into the aisle, and super-confidently walked (sauntered?) his test papers to the nun's desk in the front of the room. Then hurriedly returned to his desk. He had about thirty-five minutes or so before all the kids finished the test. This was the quiet, private time he loved most because, undisturbed, he could draw his World War II fighter planes.

Hellcats, Mustangs, Corsairs, Lightenings, Thunderbolts, Spitfires, he knew them all and loved them all. He was intense about accuracy. He was a technician.

He was Milton Caniff with a well-chewed number two pencil.

Instinctively he knew the nuns were mothers who secretly cherished the boys who were a little edgy, imaginative, challenging. As long as they were smart.

The nuns had no love for knuckleheads.

They would acknowledge that knuckleheads were made in the image and likeness of God, but in the context of a crowded classroom...they took up space. Every class had three or four kids who just showed up, and, the nun's deep and abiding Christian faith notwithstanding, in a class of forty-five kids they had no time to teach the un-teachable.

No time to attempt to break open locked doors.

But they rushed into open minds and filled them. That was their joy.

To the Dominican nuns, teaching was everything. It was a single-minded dedication. Teach, eat, pray, sleep, teach. That was the sum total of their lives. And EB and his peers were the beneficiaries of that austere, ascetic vocation.

Which is not to say that everything was perfect.

They did have those triangular rulers.

Yes, the nuns were tough.

They had to be...to control the large classes they were forced to work with. Discipline was strict, but there were laughs and lighter moments. To EB, the nuns were mothers in fourteenth century costumes.

The nuns gave to the kids an intense devotion, caring, patience, competence, humor, and a sense of family. And the kids (most of them) gave back a seriousness of purpose, an acceptance of the rules, and a willingness to work.

Symbiosis.

This was the '40s and '50s...the Golden Age. These kids were used to observing the rules. They brought that discipline with them from their homes and from the streets. The only difference was the context. In school, instead of their parents or their peers, the nuns made the rules. And all these kids respected and, for the most part, observed the rules. Even the wiseguys who couldn't resist trying to circumnavigate them.

The school year consisted of the traditional two semesters. The "A" semester began in September and ended in January. The "B" began in February and ended at the end of June. At St. Vincent Ferrer, the "A" class rooms were on the north side of the building and the "B" classes on the south. All the rooms looked exactly alike. They were the typical classroom shape, a slightly elongated rectangle with the teacher's desk in front and an enclosed cloakroom at the rear. The desks were permanently installed, that is, interlocked and not movable. There were forty-eight desks in each room. Six rows of eight, interconnected, immovable desks separated by narrow aisles. In the upper right hand corner of each desk there was an inkwell. In the upper classes when all the kids had their own fountain pens, the inkwells went unused.

Except by Gilbert McNally, who loved to pull out the little jar containing the blue-black liquid and drink it down...to the amusement of the girls who sat around him.

A class clown, but not in the wiseguy mold.

St. Vincent Ferrer School never shut down. Really, it just never closed. Today's "weather days" would cause a great deal of mirth among the Dominicans. And invoke a condescending disdain. St. Vincent Ferrer was more reliable than the U.S. Post Office.

The nuns lived in the convent that was attached to the school. So weather didn't bother them. The kids all walked to school, so weather wasn't expected to bother them.

EB remembers one day when the school closed for the afternoon. (One afternoon in eight years!) And he didn't know it until he returned after lunch and was greeted at the schoolyard door by a nun who told him to go home.

Gee, what a surprise. It was only a fourteen-inch snowfall.

For the five months of each semester, that classroom was your world. A world ruled by a benevolent dictator, if you were lucky. A malevolent dictator if you were not.

But a dictator either way.

The day was structured by subject: English, arithmetic, religion in the morning; history, social studies, music or art in the afternoon. There was a special music teacher, but all the other subjects were taught by the nun who was assigned to your class for that semester. Some revisionists question how one nun could have mastered all those subjects, but EB would defend the nuns with the observation that most of the important things he knows he learned in grammer school. (Extreme, but thought-provoking.)

There were three nuns that stand out in EB's memory; Sister Mary Edna, Sister Marita, and Sister Theresa Marie. He had a sneaky, never-admitted, little-boy crush on each of the first two, and a life-long, deep respect for the third. Of course, it was hard to think of the nuns as women, disguised as they were by their "habits" (which was the idea).

They all wore winter-white, floor-length gowns loosely waisted with over-sized black rosary beads that were tied on the left side and hung down to around knee length and ended in a giant silver and black crucifix. The gown topped a pair of "Grandma shoes", clunky, lace-up, polished black shoes with

110

thick, half-inch heels. There was an additional cape-like flap across the bodice in the same white material. On their heads they wore a black veil that curved around their faces to the shoulders, then curved again around the back and ended in the middle of the leg (we dare not say "thigh"). Under the veil was a white cap that fit tightly around the face. It came down to just above the eyebrows, followed the cheekbones down, and cinched under the chin. It hid any suggestion of a woman's hair. So, what you had basically was a discombobulated face from the eyebrows down to the chin floating in a sea of white and black. Not a person, not a woman. A nun.

EB had Sister Mary Edna in the 2A, 4A, and 7A. He thought she had a pretty face and he knew she liked him even though he was a challenge. Or maybe because he was a challenge. She was young (at least he thought so; it was hard to tell) and dynamic. Energetic and dangerously mercurial. She taught hard, she laughed hard, and she hit hard.

EB's kind of woman.

One day in the 7A, the kids were lined up to exit the class at lunch time. Sister was vexed about something or other and told the kids to keep absolute silence...NOT A SOUND!...she said.

So EB turned to the kid next to him and made a wiseguy comment about the impossibility of absolute silence.

Sister was on him in a nanosecond.

Whack!

She smacked him on the side of the head, lifted him off his feet, and slammed him into the thick, carved molding of the doorjamb.

EB bounced back into his place in line, still on his feet, but semi-conscious. Sister was in his face going on about sounds and silences and basically holding him up and he didn't hear any of that. He was simply waiting for his head to clear. When it did, he became aware that his head was doing a Pinocchio. There was a lump just above his temple that was growing at about an inch a second. The more he concentrated on it, the faster it seemed to grow. None of the other kids moved, looked, or made a sound. The girls had that smug, know-it-all look they always had when one of the boys was nailed. The boys were all scared out of their minds. They didn't want this turned into a feeding frenzy, so they all shrank down into their shirt collars and took a low profile.

Sister Mary Edna, now assured that EB was conscious and functioning, made one last comment to EB about it all being his own fault for opening his big mouth and dismissed the class for lunch.

When EB got home and his mother couldn't help but notice the ever-lengthening Pinocchio-nose lump on the side of his head, did she get hysterical? Did she insist on going back to school to conference with Sister Mary Edna? Did she threaten to sue the school for cruel and unusual punishment?

Hell, no.

His mother threatened to whack him on the other side of the head.

This was the down side of the Golden Age.

Mothers always assumed the kid was at fault. And deserved what he got. And questioned whether what he got was enough.

It was called taking responsibility for your own actions.

And, of course, the kids had their own code. You didn't complain, you didn't explain, you took your punishment like a man. Because 99% of the time, it was your own fault.

When he returned to school after lunch, Sister Mary Edna actually sought him out in the schoolyard and inquired about his good health. And snuck a peek at the new appendage added to the side of EB's head.

Very unusual. Unheard of. She was sorry.

He appreciated that. It wasn't the first time he got whacked in school and it wouldn't be the last, but it wasn't very often that the whacker showed the whackee some humanity.

He thought that should be a permanent part of the game.

Sister Marita was different.

EB had her in 2B, 4B, and as a substitute in 7B.

She was gentle. She had soft, hazel, limpid eyes and a beautifully shaped face. She was quiet, serene. Untroubled. Sister Marita might have been even younger than Sister Mary Edna but, again, it was hard to tell. What Mary Edna accomplished with bombast, Marita accomplished with serenity.

One afternoon in the 4B, Sister Marita was preoccupied in the front of the classroom, and EB, who sat near the rear, was fooling around. He was tying and retying his tie, claiming to a few of the girls who sat around him that he could do it in ten seconds or less. He had them timing each effort and tittering away. They thought it was funny, so EB thought it was hilarious.

Naturally, he got caught.

Sister Marita, ignoring the girls completely, called EB up to the front of the room and handed him a card containing the times table for the number four.

WRITE THAT ONE HUNDRED TIMES BY TOMORROW MORNING...EB accepted the card with an exaggerated, courtly bow he had just seen in a Paul Henried movie called "The Spanish Main."

The class laughed.

TWO HUNDRED TIMES...said Sister Marita very quietly.

EB bowed again.

The class laughed again.

FOUR HUNDRED TIMES...whispered Sister Marita.

The wiseguy stood stock still, knowing the next one would be eight hundred.

So, wisely he capitulated.

YES, SISTER...he said respectfully. And stayed up half the night paying his debt to society.

Sister Marita was different.

She gently punished you severely.

Then there was "Terrible Tessie".

Sister Theresa Marie taught 8A. She was a living legend. Reputed to be the toughest Dominican nun in the United States of America. In St. Vincent Ferrer, you started hearing about her in first grade. By the fifth grade, you were fearing for your life and asking your parents to move to Ohio. By the seventh grade, every thought of the coming year made some kids call in sick.

She was volcanic; she was cruel; she was the quintessential malevolent dictator. She was Hitler reincarnated. She was totally intimidating.

That's what they said.

When he reached the 8A, EB found her to be wonderful. He thought she was the quintessential pussycat. Sister Theresa Marie's job was to begin preparing the kids for high school. And that she did. She was the best math, history, social studies teacher in the school. But she was the best English teacher in the world. When EB says the most important things he knows he learned in grammar school (one of his favorite phrases), he really means the short five months in "Terrible Tessie's" class.

She was inspirational.

She instilled in EB and the other kids her own passion for the English language. She drilled them everyday on the now-lost art of declining a sentence (subject, predicate, object, subordinate clause). She beat into them a healthy respect for spelling and grammar. But above all, she made them read.

And she read to them.

She read three or four books that semester.

EB especially remembers *The Secret Garden*. She started that classic children's book around the middle of the term and she read a chapter every afternoon. She read it slowly, emotionally. On those afternoons in grade 8A, there was not a sound to be heard except the mellifluous, utterly respectful reading voice of Sister Theresa Marie...known behind her back as "Terrible Tessie".

To EB, she was the opposite of terrible.

And finally there was Sister Austina.

Sister Austina taught the 8B.

She was not a living legend.

Her job was to complete the preparation for high school. Her job was to build on Sister Theresa Marie's foundation. But she was not the teacher "Terrible Tessie" was, and she was smart enough to know it.

So she didn't try to be.

Instead, she had EB and his classmates spend the most part of the 8B taking high school entrance tests from the recent past. That's how Sister Austina taught her 8B classes.

And it was pretty smart.

Sister Austina assumed that in the previous seven and a half years the kids had learned all they were going to learn. Or at least all they needed to learn to gain entrance to high school. So her job was not to teach, per se, but to get the class comfortable with the tension of taking the high school entrance tests. And to build the kids' confidence and prepare them psychologically for the rigors of test taking. So, everyday without fail, she gave EB's class a new/old entrance test. Every day. Over and over.

After awhile, the kids greeted the tests as old friends.

Smart.

She covered all the bases. They took the tests of Brooklyn Tech, Brooklyn Prep, St. Francis Prep, Regis, Xavier, and the diocesan high school, St. Augustine.

St. Augustine was the only school from that list that EB was interested in. It was the only school that was possible for him. Augustine was a scholarship school only, so it was tuition-free. EB's parents could not afford to pay for high school. The brutal truth was they could barely afford St. Augustine because even in a free school, there were some attendant costs like books, supplies, and transportation. But they agreed he could go, if he made it.

If he got the scholarship.

EB wanted this badly.

All the boys in the class with any academic standing whatever wanted to go to a Catholic high school. That was a given. That was another aspect of the code. The alternative was Midwood High School, and that was unthinkable for a St. Vincent Ferrer kid with a 93%-94% average.

Midwood was for the knuckleheads, not for the academic elite. Not for the anointed ones. Not for the self-anointed ones, either.

That was the way it was.

St. Augustine was the only hope EB had.

That was the way it was, too.

EB understood the situation perfectly. St. Augustine was one of the two boys-only scholarship high schools for the Diocese of Brooklyn. (Bishop Loughlin was the other.) Only three boys from each parish in the southern area of Brooklyn were accepted into the school. And there were about forty parishes in that part of Brooklyn. So the competition would be fierce.

And the odds were frightening.

But competition was something he was used to, and besides, he had one more thing going for him, a more important competition motivating him, pushing him, challenging him.

Six months earlier, his cousin Matty earned a scholarship to St. Augustine.

Matty was in.

If Matty could do it, so could he.

That was always the way it was.

So EB got to work.

He worked hard on Sister Austina's practice tests. He studied all the tests looking for clues, tendencies, repeats, and he begged Austina for more and more St. Augustine tests of the past. (He never asked where she got all these old tests, nobody did; but the suspicion among the kids was that this was somehow slightly shady.) When the time came, he even traveled to Brooklyn Prep and Regis to take their tests live, even though he could never attend either school. It was good practice.

He worked hard.

He studied hard.

And he prayed hard.

He said rosaries, offered his communions, begged, pleaded, pledged himself to godliness, and committed himself to everybody in Heaven above...if only his prayers could be answered. His mother and his sister Dorothy were praying for him. At the same time, his cousin Barbara (Sister Mary Barbara) was making a novena for his cause. If Heaven would listen to anybody, it would be Barbara, he thought, when he found out she was praying for him. While he continued to pray, he continued to study.

Prayers could work miracles, but the Good Lord still demanded that you do your share.

In early June, very close to his fourteenth birthday, EB took the test for St. Augustine. Every eighth grade boy in southern Brooklyn took the test for Augustine on that day.

Let the competition begin.

EB swears to this day that he got 100%.

It's possible.

Afterward, Sister Austina went over the test with the class. So EB knew that he answered all the questions correctly. The only unknown was the essay part of the test. It was worth ten points. It was a wide-open opportunity. The kids could write a minimum of five hundred words about anything they chose, as

116

long as it dealt with family life.

Of course, it was designed to be the tie-breaker.

EB created what he described as a tear-jerking tale of family trauma. A mother's engagement ring lost while fumbling with gloves and a front door key in a blinding snowstorm. Tears. Heartbreak. Loss. But in early spring...a miracle. EB makes a snowball on his front lawn, sees something gleaming from its side, and rediscovers his mother's ring. The end.

Was that little story worth ten points? The world will never know, since test scores were never revealed. But considering that the grading of the essay could only be subjective, it's possible.

It's possible.

In mid-June of 1948, Sister Austina had the names of the three boys who would go to St. Augustine High School.

She stood in the front of the class with three cards in her hand. And dramatically put her finger to her lips.

Silence in the room.

Nobody moved. This was the highlight of the year. These were scholarships.

This was big.

EB held his breath.

She read the first two names slowly, smiling after each, allowing the class time to applaud between the names. As she called their names, the boys stood. EB was happy, and unhappy, for his classmates.

He had one more shot.

Before the third name, Sister Austina once again paused dramatically. Clearly, by the face she made, this was not her favorite moment.

The third name was EB's.

The class applauded hesitantly, puzzled by Austina's attitude and afraid to do the wrong thing. EB's friends in the class kept up a scattered applause until they became too obvious and that too petered out.

EB, too, was puzzled by Sister Austina's anti-EB attitude. Austina was not Mary Edna, Marita, or Theresa Marie. She was not challenged by wiseguys. She was not drawn to the edgy kids. She was more the nerdy type. She had never shown any love for

EB, but, up until now, she had not exhibited any hostility toward him, either.

He was standing there, embarrassed.

He was a little upset. No, very upset. His face was flushed and burning. He felt betrayed. He was hurt. He was confused. He couldn't understand it.

But he was soon to be enlightened.

It was about a half hour later, around eleven o'clock in the morning, when Sister Austina called his name and beckoned him to the front of the room. As he approached, she motioned for him to join her outside the classroom in the hallway. As he exited the door, he saw Sister Mary Florence, who was the principal of the school. That was a surprise. Oh, oh, this can't be good, he thought. Now he faced the two nuns in the hallway outside the now closed door of the 8B, his last classroom at St. Vincent Ferrer. WE CANNOT ALLOW YOU TO ACCEPT THIS SCHOL-ARSHIP...said Sister Austina.

What??

What the hell...excuse me, heck...was going on here?...he was stunned. He was numbed. He looked at the two nuns. First they were glaring at him, then their faces softened, and then they were imploring him...WE BOTH WANTED THIS SCHOLAR-SHIP TO GO TO ONE OF THE MORE...ER....DEPENDABLE BOYS...ER...ONE OF THE MORE STUDIOUS BOYS IN THE CLASS...said Mary Florence...FOR THE SAKE OF ST. VINCENT FERRER....added Mary Florence...YOU'RE ONE OF THOSE PEASE'S BOYS...said Austina...YOU HANG OUT WITH THOSE LOWLIFE BOYS WHO SMOKE, AND CURSE...continued Austina...AND PRETTY SOON YOU'LL BE DOING ALL THOSE THINGS YOURSELF, IF YOU ARE NOT ALREADY DOING SO...finished Austina.

My God! This is a nightmare! After all that work, after all that studying, after all that praying! This is un-Christian. This is blasphemy...FIRST IT WAS YOUR COUSIN, MATTHEW, NOW YOU...FRANKLY, WE FEAR THAT BOTH OF YOU WILL THROW AWAY YOUR SCHOLARSHIPS IN SHORT ORDER... WE SHOULD HAVE STOPPED MATTHEW...IT'S TOO LATE NOW, BUT WE CANNOT ALLOW THIS TO HAPPEN AGAIN...said Austina...YOU MUST FORSAKE THIS SCHOL-

118

ARSHIP...FOR THE SAKE OF YOUR PARISH...finished Austina...WE DARE NOT EMBARRASS OUR PARISH...added Mary Florence.

EB was recovering his equilibrium. His cheeks were starting to burn in a different way. You didn't get angry at the nuns, at least not to their faces, but he was getting close. He stared back at the two nuns. He was thirteen; they were both in their fifties. A mis-match. But his mind was working furiously...SISTERS, YOU CAN'T DO THIS...YOU DON'T HAVE THE AUTHORITY... THIS IS A DIOCESAN MATTER...THIS IS THE BISHOP'S BUSINESS...

A mistake.

A challenge to their authority...dumb!

Sister Austina jumped on it...DON'T BE DISRESPECTFUL...AND DON'T BE STUPID...OF COURSE WE HAVE THE AUTHORITY...THE BISHOP'S OFFICE RELIES ON OUR EVALUATIONS OF OUR OWN STUDENTS...THE RESULTS OF THE TEST CAN BE OVERRULED IF THAT IS OUR RECOMMENDATION...THE DIOCESAN SCHOOLS HAVE REPUTATIONS TO PROTECT, TOO...(pause)...WE ARE TRULY SORRY, THIS IS OUR DECISION...THIS IS OUR WISH...

He was losing ground. No more mistakes or he was done. Thinking, thinking, thinking...maybe...maybe...he looked Sister Austina right in the eye, then he looked Sister Mary Florence right in the eye, then he put his head down and, with all the sincere respect he could muster, he said in a hushed voice...SISTERS, I UNDERSTAND YOUR CONCERNS AND I UNDERSTAND THAT THIS IS YOUR WISH...(double pause)...BUT WHAT ABOUT GOD'S WISH?...WHAT ABOUT GOD'S WILL?...They looked at him, not comprehending. If he ever had a twinkle in his eye, it was now, as he explained...SISTERS, I WORKED VERY HARD FOR THIS, I STUDIED VERY HARD FOR THIS, BUT I KNEW THAT WASN'T ENOUGH...SO I PRAYED VERY HARD, TOO...MY MOM PRAYED FOR ME...MY SISTER SAID THE ROSARY FOR ME EVERY DAY...MY COUSIN BARBARA DID A NOVENA FOR ME...AND ALL THOSE PRAYERS WERE ANSWERED...SO ISN'T THIS GOD'S WILL?...ISN'T IT GOD'S WILL THAT I GO TO ST. AUGUSTINE?...The two nuns looked at him in complete, stunned silence.

It was everything they had ever taught him. He had

learned his lessons well.

Sister Austina's look turned into a glare.

But Sister Mary Florence's face softened, her eyes glistened, she put her hand to her mouth and tried mightily, but unsuccessfully, to stifle a smile. Then EB knew he was all right.

She was after all, the principal of the school.

Days later, he began to understand that they were probably running a bluff on him. Trying to scare him into committing himself to working hard in high school. Consistently hard, as he had never done at St. Vincent Ferrer. And also to scare him into making a life style change away from Pease's candy store and its corrupting influences.

That was not going to happen.

Soon (too soon) he was to discover how prescient the nuns really were. How right they were to worry about him. How right they were about everything.

But that's why they were nuns.

Worrying about kids was their vocation.

And they were good at it.

Chapter Fourteen-St. Augustine **14**

St. Augustine was different from St. Vincent Ferrer.

It follows...it was a high school.

But the similarities were striking.

It follows...it was a diocesan high school.

The physical classrooms were almost exactly the same: the same size, the same shape, with the same desks, the same blackboards, the same windows, the same teachers' desks in the same locations. And like St. Vincent Ferrer, the students stayed in the same classroom all day. They stayed and sat and stayed and sat...and the teachers came to them.

And finally, it follows that the teachers were very different...but disappointingly familiar. These teachers were men. But they were men in long, ankle-length black cassocks and distinctive nun-like white collars.

Christian Brothers.

Tough, no-nonsense, serious men with short fuses.

Dedicated disciplinarians with a zealot-like passion for physical enforcement. Stern, grown men who were surrounded by hundreds of pubescent, book-smart and street-smart Brooklyn wiseguys. And none too happy about it. So they were not about to take any crap from any smart-ass kid. There was a lot of Rikers Island in St. Augustine High School.

St. Augustine High School existed in another world from EB's Flatbush neighborhood. It was located on Park Place and 6th Avenue in downtown Brooklyn, not far from the Bergen Street stop on the IRT subway. This was a much grittier neighborhood. There were few trees, little grass, but a whole lot of cement. Well trod cement. Cracked cement. Old cement. Downtown Brooklyn was a much older area than Flatbush, and in the late forties it was starting to show its age.

And speaking of showing some age, EB was two months past his fourteenth birthday in September of 1948 when he entered his new high school for the first time. That morning, he traveled with his friends from the neighborhood; Bobby Waegelein, Jerry Frost, his cousin Matty, and Eddie Bohan (BO-wen, no relation to Bud Bo-HAN). All those boys were a class ahead of EB and they had the routine worked out from the previous semester. They met on the corner of East 37th and Glenwood Avenue at exactly 7:45AM. They came from all directions, but that location was central for all. If anybody was more than three minutes late, the others did not wait. That was the rule and, as always, strictly enforced.

Eddie Mitchell also attended St. Augustine, but he was never counted on to be in the traveling group. Meeting a time deadline was never Eddie Mitchell's forte. A three-minute window was too narrow for him. A twenty-minute window was asking a lot of Eddie Mitchell. How he managed to get to school on time was one of the great mysteries of the Golden Age.

From the corner of 37th Street, the boys walked down Glenwood Road to Flatbush Avenue (about ten minutes) and boarded an IRT subway train. They never used the seats. Rather, they stood in the vestibule of the last car. It was like a room of their own. It was always the last car so their friends from other parishes who boarded the train along the way would know where to find them. On some mornings, it got pretty crowded in that vestibule. And very chatty. Jerry Frost exited the train at the President Street station to go to Brooklyn Prep. Bobby Waegelein and Eddie Bohan stayed on with EB and Matty for the whole twenty-five minute ride to Bergen Street. They both attended St. Francis Prep, which was nearby.

The boys walked that route everyday come rainstorms, snowstorms, hailstorms, or windstorms...whether it was freezing cold or unbearably hot.

There was never a car, never a ride.

It never dawned on them to whine about it. That's the way it was. If the weather was really fierce, there was a bus on Glenwood Road that they could take to Flatbush Avenue. But that was a rare occurrence.

It cost money.

EB's first year at St. Augustine was successful. And, for him, relatively uneventful. His grade average at the end of his first year was 87%. His mom thought that was fine, but secretly EB was a little embarrassed. It was the first time in his school life that his average dropped under 90%.

To EB, 87% was heading toward knucklehead territory.

And that bothered him at the end of his first year of high school. It also bothered him that his days of coasting were over. The 87% made it clear this was going to be work. He also had to stay out of trouble. And for the most part, he did.

He got caught smoking in the gym after lunch a couple of times during the first weeks of school, but that was not considered a serious infraction. It was a well-known game of hide-and-seek with the vice-principal.

The gym was right next to the cafeteria, and after lunch, all the wiseguys wandered to the back of the basketball court, hid behind some pillars, and lit up. Of course, the vice-principal knew that and tried all manner of tricks to sneak up on the perpetrators. It was all rather good natured. If caught, it brought a punch to the arm or a whack on the head and the confiscation of the cigarette pack. That last was a serious loss, so these super-smart scholarship winners put their analytical minds against that problem in a hurry.

Their solution was simple. After the first week, they only carried a few "loosies" to the lunchroom and kept their packs safely tucked away in their lockers.

Thus, the games began.

EB made new friends from parishes all over the southern half of Brooklyn...parishes he had never heard of. He met a couple of kids from as far away as Far Rockaway (which was the borough of Queens). How they managed to get into a Brooklyn diocesan high school was another one of those mysteries of Church politics that nobody talked about or questioned.

His freshman year consisted of three classes of about forty-five kids per class. They were told that was the largest class ever accepted into St. Augustine; until the class of September 1948, all years had a maximum of two classes. To EB, his own class was just about the same size as his class at St. Vincent Ferrer, so it didn't seem like a big deal. But EB missed the point. To the teachers, it wasn't the size of the class that mattered; they could manage fifty kids with their iron-fisted discipline. No, to the brothers it was the number of classes that was unmanageable. Three classes instead of two increased their daily work load by a third.

To the Christian Brothers, a three-class year was a very big deal.

A big bad deal.

They were vocal in their intent to whittle it down to a more manageable size. They openly threatened to cut the three classes down to two. And, eventually, they would do just that.

At St. Augustine High School, there were no electives. The courses you elected to take were the courses the school told you to take. Simple and straightforward. No election necessary.

No kvetching allowed.

So you elected Latin, English, algebra, history, biology, and religion... and liked it.

That was a heavy load. And during his freshman year, EB handled it well. He enjoyed Latin, he had an affinity for it (it was a Catholic thing). His orderly, problem-solving mind was tailor-made for the symmetry of algebra. He was mostly serious in the classroom and did his homework. Even though it was a drag on his social life. During his freshman year, he stayed home after supper and did his homework even though he wanted to be around the corner at the candy store with his friends. They were seasoned high school veterans, second semester freshman or sophomores, and they were all there every night, telling stories, arguing sports, smoking, planning, spitting, laughing, and he just knew he was missing everything. The pull was almost irresistible.

But resist it he did.

The first year.

The second semester of sophomore year was the beginning of the end. At home, EB was no longer resisting the peer pressure of every day night life. He was fifteen years old and he was out till ten or eleven o'clock almost every night with his friends. They stayed in Pease's candy store or they traveled to other hangouts in nearby parishes to meet girls, girls they knew from the Farragut Pool, girls they knew from school dances, or girls they didn't know at all but hoped to.

At school, EB was introduced to French, physics, and geometry. Subjects that demanded work, study, memorization. Subjects that demanded time. And time was the one thing that EB couldn't or wouldn't give them.

At the end of EB's first semester of his sophomore year, his cousin Matty dropped out of St. Augustine.

Oh my God...don't tell Sister Austina.

Never mind, she already knows.

She always knew.

At this time, EB's class was earning a bad reputation among the teaching staff. Among the Christian Brothers, it was seen as a class with more than its share of screw-ups and troublemakers. A class to be watched.

One afternoon early in the second semester of the sophomore year, EB's class was scheduled for a Latin class, but no teacher showed up. The class waited. And waited. And grew restless. And no teacher came.

The class figured no one was watching.

Somebody threw an eraser; somebody threw it back. And they were off. A full-fledged chalk and eraser fight. Whoops and hollers. Laughs and chaos. But this was the class to be watched, so, of course, they were watching. The office had assigned a substitute teacher and he walked into the room in the middle of all of this. When Brother Leo entered the room and saw the chaos, he was upset. But when he was hit in the neck with a wayward eraser, he was pissed off.

And pissing off Brother Leo was not a good thing to do.

Leo was only average in height but burly, muscular. The scuttlebutt was that he was a fighter, a boxer, before the took his vows and became a Christian Brother.

And he looked the part.

Leo was also one of the quietest of the brothers in the school. The kids viewed him as one of the good guys. They saw him as approachable and friendly, but they also saw him as intense, brooding, smoldering.

And that worried them.

When the entire class finally realized that Brother Leo had entered the room, forty kids as if they were one dove back into their seats. And an anticipatory silence fell over the room. And Brother Leo maintained it. He didn't say a word. He went to the desk in the front of the room, sat down and put his head in his hands, staring at the desktop. He stayed that way for five minutes. Not moving except to wring his hands emotionally and occasionally to shake a little in intense thought, or prayer. Or whatever he was doing, or thinking.

Five minutes and not a sound from the class.

Or from Brother Leo.

It was frightening.

Then he came out of it. Stood up, moved to the center aisle, and told the class to line up in single file, starting right in front of him and going back and around the room. Brother Leo then slapped the face of the first kid in line. It sounded like a rifle shot in the silent room. He smacked him hard with an open hand. And told him to return to his seat. Then he slapped the next kid. And the next, and the next.

EB's turn came and he stood there, not wavering, not cowering, true to the code. He did set his feet because the last thing he wanted to do was to lose his balance. How wimpy that would have been. How embarrassing that would have been.

The slap came. It hurt for an instant. Then it was over.

And he returned to his seat.

Brother Leo whacked all forty plus kids in the class, except one. He made the smallest kid in the class lean over one of the desks and he spanked him. Once.

Christian Brother compassion.

Although EB didn't think Leo did the kid a favor. He found it a little humiliating. And later the kid told him he felt the same way.

The class was seated in total, absolute silence. Brother Leo returned to the teacher's desk and chair and resumed his position. Head in hands and still shaking with emotion. It wasn't over yet.

Finally, after many long minutes that to the kids seemed like hours, Brother Leo rose and walked to the window side of the room. He reached for the long window pole, put it across his shoulders, looped his arms over it and again moved to the center of the room. Now this pole had a diameter of at least two inches. It was ten feet long. It was made of good, solid, golden oak. It was thick, it was strong, it was unyielding.

Like Brother Leo.

He started to exert downward pressure with his arms. He strained, his face contorted. The pole bent, but did not...would not...break. Brother Leo's face reddened, his arms went into mini-spasms as he strained with all his considerable might. His body bent with the effort.

The pole snapped across his shoulders.

He picked up the two pieces of broken pole, walked to the window, opened the lower section, and threw the pieces out the window. Then he slowly turned and faced the class and spoke his first words...BETTER TO BREAK ONE POLE THAN ALL OF YOUR HEADS.

Geezus!

EB was enthralled. Spellbound. What a performance! He was scared silly, but he was so into it he wanted to applaud.

Of course, he knew better. He knew that he dare not do anything like that...or he would get a severely broken head. But he couldn't get over it. Brother Leo was now talking to them, conciliatory, avuncular, advising them. They were getting to be known as a class of screw-ups. Not all, but the bad apples were polluting the barrel. And if they didn't change it, square themselves away, they were in for big trouble. The brothers were offering their help, but the students, the good guys, had to seek it, reach out for it. He urged them to do just that. Before it was too late.

But EB wasn't really listening.

What an experience! It was like a movie. Yeah, it was a John Wayne movie. Only the Duke could make his point as dramatically as that. Yeah, Brother Leo was John Wayne.

EB was impressed.

But not listening.

EB' sophomore year ended in June 1950. His grades were not only low, they were beneath him. And he knew it. During the last semester of this sophomore year, he did his homework during study periods, or he didn't do it at all. He played hooky five or six times with Bobby Waegelein, or Red Wallace, or some of the other kids in his class. Every morning after exiting the IRT, Bobby, EB, Red Wallace, Eddie Bohan, and Billy Lyons, would stop in the Rainbow Coffee Shop to sip a cup of coffee and plot the day's activities. Activities that all too often did not allow time for going to classes.

On those days, they would walk downtown and go to the Paramount Theatre, or the Fox, or walk the other way to Prospect Park. Or take the subway back to the neighborhood and go to the College Movie to see a re-release ("Guadulcanal Diary," "The Purple Heart," the Tarzan series, the Marx Brothers).

In June of 1950, at the end of his sophomore year, EB was in academic trouble and he was well aware of it. But he wasn't inclined to do much about it. He was throwing away a scholarship and he felt terrible about that. But he rationalized away the guilt. He told himself that the tight, overbearing, unrelenting Catholic school discipline was getting to him after all these years. He needed freedom, he lied to himself.

Freedom like his cousin Matty had, and Ed Stuchbury, Billy Hill, Billy Leddy and Jack Noonan and all the other guys he knew in Midwood. They were getting away with murder and he was still getting whacked around.

He needed a break, he needed some peace.

Peace, and freedom, that's what he needed.

And now the unthinkable was allowed, or welcomed, into his thinking. Now the impossible was a possibility. Now Midwood High School was a viable alternative. Now Midwood was the solution to his problems. Peace, and freedom, that's what he needed.

His head was working overtime...but his heart was taking a few years off.

At the end of June 1950, a few weeks after EB's sophomore semester ended, his sister Dorothy graduated from St. Vincent Ferrer. It was her big day and there was a small celebration at their house.

That's where EB was when he first heard of the North Korean invasion of South Korea and President Truman's immediate call for a "police action". Later that night when the celebration was winding down, EB was sitting alone on their front stoop. Dorothy joined him there and they talked quietly about the implications of Truman's decision. EB was a few days short of his sixteenth birthday, and on that night his patriotic fervor was in overdrive. If this is a real war, he told her, he would enlist as soon as he was old enough.

After all, his was the last generation that believed war was romantic. John Wayne, Dana Andrews, William Bendix, Robert Taylor, and the Hollywood directors like John Ford had done their job well.

For the kids of this United States of America, war was manly, honorable, right, and just. EB and his friends believed it was their job to right the wrongs of the world. To punish the evil-doers was their responsibility.

The code.

Only bigger.

EB and all his friends were believers. They didn't agree on everything, but they were of one mind on the subject of war.

Any kid who thought that a P-51 Mustang was the most beautiful thing he had ever seen this side of Jenny O'Halloran was definitely brainwashed.

And ready to go.

They were too young for World War II. That war belonged

to older brothers, uncles, and cousins.

This one would be theirs.

When EB and his classmates returned to St. Augustine in September to begin their junior year, they found that there were some changes made.

Ominous changes.

The brothers had done a fast shuffle over the summer. They took the wiseguys from all three classes and grouped them together in the same class. Now there were two classes of straight, smiling, upright citizens, and one class that was filled with a bunch of iconoclasts, malcontents, system-beaters, slackers, unmanageable minds, and wasted talents.

The damned.

The doomed.

And, of course, EB was one of them.

The brothers made no secret of their motives. They predicted that 50% of them would be gone by the end of the semester. They said that was the method to their madness. They said the outcome was inevitable. The barrel was now full of bad apples. And the apples would rot each other.

Unless.

Unless...they confessed their sins, said a heartfelt act of contrition, and petitioned the brothers for help. The brothers would help, wanted to help, but had to be asked by the whole class. That is, the class as a unit. One entity. One voice.

No way.

A lot of strange things happened that semester. The kids were unyielding. The system was equally adamant...so things deteriorated quickly.

The class had a lay teacher (that is, a man who didn't wear a cassock, wasn't a brother, didn't take a vow of chastity, and at night went home to a wife and children) who taught math and one day brought up the "situation" in a speech he had no business making...YOU ARE A BUNCH OF JERKS...YOU HAVE NO RESPECT FOR ANYTHING...YOU WERE HANDED THE GIFT OF A SCHOLARSHIP AND YOU ARE ABOUT TO THROW IT AWAY...OBVIOUSLY, YOU HAVE THE BRAINS... SO YOU'RE

NOT JUST JERKS, YOU'RE THIEVES...YOU STOLE SOME-
BODY ELSE'S RIGHT TO A FREE EDUCATION...THE BROTH-
ERS ARE RIGHT, OF COURSE...AND THEY WILL SUCCEED IN
GETTING RID OF YOU DEADBEATS...he said.

The class did not like that speech.

It's not that the man was wrong; it's just that in the considered opinion of EB's by now paranoid class, he didn't have the
right to make the speech. He wasn't a brother. He was just a math
teacher in mufti. If he didn't like them, they didn't much care;
they didn't like him, either.

So the next day when he entered the class, they all turned
in unison and faced the back of the room. And stayed that way
for the entire fifty-minute class.

And the next day they did the same thing.

The following day, the system (impersonal, invisible)
replaced him with a brother, and that was the end of that.

The substitute teacher was a brother whose name was
Alban Anthony. He was a small, frail man. Effete. Ascetic. He
spoke in a strange, soft voice that was barely above a whisper.
And he had an abnormally large elongated head. Hence, his nickname: Bullet Head. But these kids had learned a long time ago
not to be misled by physical appearances.

Bullet Head was dangerous.

In this, his junior year, EB was seated three desks from the
front of the room in the last aisle on the right (from the student's
perspective, facing the teacher). Next to him on his right, across
a narrow aisle, was a wall of steel lockers. In the desk directly in
front of EB was a kid named Fitzpatrick. He was a wiseguy in
good standing, having been left back at least one semester and
not making noticeable improvements in this one. One day, in the
front of the room, Brother Alban Anthony turned his back, and
Fitzpatrick gave him the arm. It was another of those now-famil-
iar situations. Silence in the room. A feeling in the room. Nobody
knew how, but Alban Anthony knew the kid did it. Later, they
discussed it endlessly. He couldn't have seen Fitzpatrick, could
he have? No, impossible. He had his back turned. There were a
few titters when Fitz flew the arm, but that wouldn't have told
brother what it was. No, it was impossible, he couldn't have seen
him.

Still...he had that weird head.

Bullet Head never turned around and looked at Fitzpatrick. But he was on the move. In the other direction. He moved slowly. He did everything slowly, softly. He reached the last aisle across the room and began moving to the rear. He glided silently across the back of the room. He reached EB's aisle and slowly turned into it. His movement slowed even more. Not a sound. He moved past EB's desk, past Fitzpatrick's desk, past the next desk, then he stopped.

EB tried to be real small in his seat. What if that extra eye in Alban Anthony's head didn't see all that well? What if that mysterious eye made a mistake and saw EB instead? Maybe it wasn't an eye after all. What if it was extra sensory perception? ESP wasn't all that accurate, right?

Think small.

Alban Anthony turned again and started slowly back up the aisle. When he came abreast of Fitzpatrick's desk, he didn't seem to stop at all. He just threw an uppercut at the kid with an open right hand that seemed to come from the floor...WHACK!...Fitzpatrick flew up and out of his seat, smashed into the lockers, and bounced back into his seat. Where he received a left cross to the head...WHACK!...that pushed him across the aisle into the next desk, which bounced him back into his seat where another uppercut...WHACK!...put him back into the lockers and back into his seat.

Bullet Head moved away. He moved slowly to the front of the room toward his desk. And stopped there for a moment, leaning hard on his hands on top of the desk. His enormous, mystical, magical head was sagging between his shoulders. He took a few deep breaths, turned and came back toward the semi-conscious Fitzpatrick. Brother was moving with a little more purpose now.

Oh Geezus, said EB to himself, what is it about these brothers? It's never over when it's over. They always come back for more. He sunk down in his seat. Everybody was sinking in his seat, making himself smaller.

The whole class now looked like a bunch of midgets.

When Brother Alban Anthony reached Fitzpatrick, he hit him just one more time. He used the uppercut...WHACK...and the kid was no more prepared for it this time than he was the first time. Again Fitzpatrick flew up and into the lockers and back into his seat.

EB was fascinated by that. No matter how hard or high Fitzpatrick hit the lockers, he always bounced back into his seat.

Pretty neat.

Oh those brothers, they were good.

Bullet Head returned to the teacher's desk in the front of the room. Through it all, he never said a word. He took a moment to gather himself, then in his little whispery, effete voice he told the class to prepare for a quiz.

That was it.

He never mentioned the incident for the rest of the semester. The class assumed he believed he made his point. And the kids agreed.

Bullet Head was dangerous.

EB knew it was over when he got a 22 on a physics test. Humiliation.

He told himself that physics was alien to his brain's wiring. It just did not compute. As soon as he finished telling himself that, he immediately told himself that that was bullshit. He hated rationalizations. And that was the worst kind of rationalization because it did not hold up. His brain had proven itself over the years.

It was a good brain.

It had never let him down. But even a good brain needed some direction.

Even a good brain needed some help, some input, some support, a vote of confidence. Something.

And right now, EB was fresh out of everything.

Through the semester, he tried to prepare his parents for the inevitable. His mom was saddened but accepting. That was her way. His father at first tried to suggest it was the brothers' fault, but EB squashed that. Finally his father, too, accepted the fact that it was over.

There were no recriminations.

They didn't yell or scream.

As always, they allowed him to make his own decisions.

They assumed he was doing what he had to do and taking the responsibility for his own actions. That's all they asked. If he had to leave St. Augustine, so be it. That's just the way it was. Midwood was a fine school, too.

In January of 1951, at the end of the first semester of his junior year, EB dropped out of St. Augustine High School.

Please...please don't tell Sister Austina.
Never mind.

Chapter Fifteen-Midwood High School # 15

Midwood High School was like a dream...in the continuum of EB's life, it was only a short, hazy sequence preceeded and succeeded by a vigorous, hard-edged reality.

Did it really happen?

He wasn't sure because he drifted through it like a spectral abstraction. He was there, but he wasn't there. Physically he showed up, but spiritually he didn't connect with Midwood. And Midwood didn't connect with him.

He simply did not care.

And for a kid who threw himself into everything he did with intense emotion and enthusiasm, these last few years were strange in the extreme. Not caring was definitely not his style.

Strange. Madness.

The Mad Years.

Following instructions from his friends (veterans of the Midwood system), he reported a week late. That was explained by informing the front office and his teachers that his old school screwed up and it took a week into the term to get all the paper work necessary to effect the transfer to his new school.

Nobody questioned that, as predicted by his wiseguy friends.

EB did have to explain his tardiness to every individual teacher on his schedule. That all went smoothly until he met his intermediate algebra teacher, an arrogant little man who, after looking through his transfer papers, insisted (even after being politely corrected) in pronouncing St. Augustine as "Saint AWW-gus-teen". Like the city in the state of Florida.

EB hated him for that.

And failed his class on purpose.

The next term, in September of 1951, the beginning of his senior year, he took intermediate algebra again with a different teacher, another male teacher whom he liked as much as he hated the other.

At the end of the semester, he had a 95% average.

When his grade advisor looked at his report card, she could not help but notice that the admirable 95 was surrounded by contemptible 65s in every other subject. When she asked him to explain that, he simply smiled and shrugged.

He was sending the messages.

It was up to them to understand them.

Midwood was located on Bedford Avenue across the street from Brooklyn College. EB could have walked there in twenty minutes. But in the morning, he boarded the Glenwood Road bus simply to save time. The bus dropped him off in front of the school, so it was very convenient. In the afternoon, usually around 2:15PM, he walked home. Or more likely to Pease's.

The day started early at Midwood. Home room was first at 8:15AM. It was primarily used for attendance, so it was quiet. Some kids slept.

And didn't get whacked for it.

A different world.

Another difference was that the kids traveled to the teachers, not vice versa. So every fifty minutes, there was a tremendous movement and energy throughout the school. The kids got to see friends from other classes, they had time to stop and chat, they had time to be social (very important in Midwood culture), and they had time to sneak a smoke (very important in EB culture). One more big difference was the existence of electives. That was a first for EB.

Choice.

Freedom.

And he had an advantage because of the heavy load he had carried at St. Augustine. In terms of credits, he was ahead of his Midwood peers, so he could afford to pick soft courses and coast from here to graduation.

Physically, EB showed up everyday.

He didn't play "the hook" very often in Midwood. He cut a class here and there, but the day was so comparatively short that there was very little reason not to stick it out.

It was easy.

And the girls were nice.

Or course, the girls were the biggest diference of all. No girls allowed in St. Augustine...no way. There were attractive girls all over Midwood High School. Italian girls, Jewish girls, Irish girls, Negro girls, Protestant girls, Catholic girls...of every size, every shape, every color, every variation the Good Lord could possibly conceive of.

And obviously, the good Lord was a conceptual genius.

It was wonderful.

To a sexually repressed Catholic kid like EB, sitting in back of a pretty girl in a translucent white blouse with show-through bra straps was a lot more pleasant than sitting in back of that Fitzpatrick kid.

And a lot safer.

There was one girl that EB noticed immediately. They shared the same lunch period and he spotted her in the first few days. She walked by as he sat with a few of this friends. She had great legs. Outstanding legs. Major league legs. Great definition. She had this little muscle that rippled down the side of her sensuously curved calf as she glided by. That subtle movement, invisible to most insensitive clod-guys, drove EB crazy.

This girl had legs like Cyd Charisse.

And that was the highest compliment he could pay to any pair of legs.

EB was not known for his poker face, therefore the girl knew she was driving him nuts. So during lunch period, she and her friends always managed to cruise in his direction...they didn't exactly walk, they kind of sailed along on an invisible, fragrant breeze to wherever he was sitting. And she and her friends always giggled loudly as they tacked by him. Did he do anything about this physical attraction?

No...of course not.

Because this girl was Italian, and somewhere in this lunchroom, or somewhere in this school, or somewhere out there on Avenue N and Ralph Avenue there was a slick-haired, weight-lifting, Mafia wannabe boyfriend who could...and would...break EB's legs.

These days, a kid had to be careful.

He really did believe that, although it was probably nonsense. Or at least greatly exaggerated. If he understood the opposite sex better than he did, he would have acted differently.

But he didn't.

And he didn't.

When his first semester in Midwood ended in June of 1951, EB was gliding along. He wasn't working at it. He was not interested. He barely passed all his courses. The teachers were carrying him because he seemed like a decent kid. He showed up. He was quiet, disinterested, inscrutable, opaque, but at least he did not cause them any trouble. (When a wiseguy isn't causing any trouble, quick, take his pulse.) Of course they knew he was coasting. That was not unusual among the expatriate Catholic school kids. If these kids, these ex-pats, wanted to become invisible, why that was entirely up to them. The New York City Board of Education teachers didn't spend a whole lot of time worrying about it.

Don't worry, be happy.

Moving into the summer of 1951, EB's mind was involved with more weighty matters.

He had just turned seventeen,.

The "police action" in Korea was now a full-fledged war. Casualties were mounting. And some of them were neighborhood boys just a year or two older than EB. To make it more heartbreaking, some of them were Pease's boys.

An obscenity.

EB and his friends were enraged.

And he was beginning to think about enlisting in the Navy.

And to hell with high school.

16 Chapter Sixteen-Saloons

In the '40s and'50s, the drinking age in New York State was eighteen. (Maybe that's one reason they called it the Golden Age.)

That meant you started drinking beer at sixteen.

Or earlier, if you could find a way.

And you could always find a way.

One of EB's first nights of drinking beer was on a warm summer night in 1949. Which is not say that this was the first time he ever drank a beer. That would not be true. But this night was significant because he was fifteen and this was his long-awaited initiation into that murky man's world of swilling steins of beer in a saloon around a table with the other guys...just laughing, smoking, cursing, talkin' sports and politics.

Heady stuff.

And addictive. As EB would discover soon enough.

On this night, Dick Duckett was in charge. This was to be another life lesson from the always unpredictable mind of Duckett who was now a few months shy of eighteen. Which, from a beer drinking point of view, was close enough to be legal. So when the boys met at Pease's in the early evening, Dick suggested (a suggestion from Dick was really a mandate) to EB, Matty, Bobby Waegelein, and Jerry Frost that it was about time that they go down to Coney Island and drink a few beers. And, Dick explained, they would do that in a saloon called Feltman's, a place so big that no one will ever question their ages. And to make sure of that, Dick, the semi-legal drinker, would go to the bar and bring pitchers back to the table so the bartenders would never see the other boys. Sounded good, as Dick's ideas always did, and off they went.

They took the Glenwood Road bus to the BMT subway train at 16th Street and Avenue M and boarded the train. The last stop on that subway line was Coney Island.

Feltman's was a world-famous (self-proclaimed) German Beer Garden and Restaurant on Surf Avenue and West Tenth Street. The property extended from Surf Avenue to the beach. Feltman's went back to the early 1900s, and was so big that it spanned a whole city block. It was close to world-famous (self-proclaimed) Steeplechase Park and its innovative Parachute Ride.

There was another wonderful ride at Steeplechase that EB and Matty loved when they were kids. It was a horse race that was absolutely unique. There were eight carousel-like wooden horses attached to iron rail tracks. You mounted your horse below the starting line and were mechanically pulled, like a roller coaster car, up to a small rise. That was the official starting line, and from there everything was left to gravity. The horses sped along, up and down, on rails that encircled the Pavilion of Fun. In length, the ride was probably no more than a half mile or so, but seemed longer. Because it was a gravity ride, you never knew which horse would win the race, although it was well known among the cognoscenti that the heaviest horse (that is, the horse carrying the heaviest load) would always win. Money was lost due to the ignorance of that immutable fact of physics.

The night at Feltman's worked just as Dick said it would. The boys sat and drank pitchers of beer for a few hours and nobody bothered them. For EB, it was his first experience of sustained drinking. And his first taste of quality German beer sipped from a stein instead of a cardboard container behind somebody's garage. This was the big time.

He liked it.

He liked everything about it.

And the boys did get a little funny-faced.

They weren't fallin' down drunk, but when they left Feltman's that night, they were definitely at the "feeling no pain" stage. Which would explain EB's two rides on the Parachute.

False courage.

Normally the Parachute was not one of his favorite rides. It went straight up, very high up (you could practically see Wyoming from the top), and fell straight down. It was kind of boring and there was no real reward for the amount of courage you had to invest.

And it was not the ride to take with a belly full of beer.

After the rides, the five boys drifted down to the beach and stretched out on the sand. It was a hot night. There were not many cool nights in a Brooklyn summer. So Duckett suggested (mandated) that they go skinny dipping. It would cool them off and help sober them up for the ride home, said Dick in his always unassailable, irresistible, Dick-logic kind of way.

So they did.

They piled their clothes on the sand close enough to the water line that they could keep their eyes on them, and plunged, buck-naked, into the Coney Island surf. Looking out into the ocean, it was dark...black. But looking back toward the beach, the light was dazzling. Coney Island was like Times Square...lights, lights, lights. And all that light spilled out onto the sand and out beyond the water line. The boys could see their clothes alright, but that meant that anyone on the beach could see the boys, too. Now skinny dipping may sound like normal activity on a steamy summer night, but this was not a secluded swimming hole somewhere in Iowa...this was Brooklyn, New York.

142

There were no swimming holes in Brooklyn.

There was only the Atlantic Ocean. And big, popular beaches like Coney Island. And on the big, popular beaches like Coney Island on summer nights, even on sweltering summer nights, Brooklyn kids usually did not go skinny dipping.

Because on sweltering summer nights in Brooklyn's Coney Island, there were approximately four hundred fifty thousand people on the beach.

And EB was certain that all of them were staring at his bare butt.

A shocking thought for a Catholic school kid.

For EB, the night at Feltman's was the beginning of a long love affair with the sociability and camaraderie of "havin' a few with the boys." For the next few years, EB and his friends drank a lot of beer. Mostly on Friday and Saturday nights. Through the fall of 1949 and the spring, summer, and fall of 1950, they had a few saloons they could drink in without getting hassled.

One of them was a place called Campbell's and McQuire's on Avenue D and 43rd Street. It gradually replaced the candy stores and ice cream parlors as the place to hang out. At least on weekend nights.

They were now a permanent group of a dozen or so male friends, with a few females who were part of the group and another half dozen girls who came and went depending on the status and strength of their romantic linkages. They were careful to keep a low profile in the bars. They stayed together in a quiet corner. No noise, no trouble, that was the game. They drank, they talked, they debated, they argued, they laughed, they got to know each other in new ways, deeper ways.

But quietly.

No fuss, no muss, no fights, no teenage bullshit.

And so they were welcome.

There was another "safehouse" bar called Osgood's on Nostrand Avenue and Avenue D. They spent a lot of time there, too. But usually later at night. That was the bar they went to after Campbell's and McQuire's. It was a more sophisticated location. It was on the perimeter of the neighborhood and, therefore, an opportunity to meet new females. So that was where they ended many a Friday or Saturday night.

EB was in Campbell's and McQuire's on a Friday night in early winter of 1950. It was about 11PM. He was sitting in their corner with a few of his friends when Jerry Frost came in and motioned to EB to join him outside. They wanted him to be a witness.

Frost, Bobby Waegelein, Harold Brice, and Ed Stuchbury had bet Ed Mitchell ten dollars that he could not chug-a-lug a pint of gin.

Ed Mitchell had, of course, accepted the bet.

They gathered in the doorway of a closed store next to the bar and prepared to watch Mitch try to win the bet...SUCKERS!...crowed Mitch...FOOLS!...WATCH AND BE AWED...THIS IS THE WAY A MAN DRINKS...HEMINGWAY COULD DO THIS...I CAN DO THIS...I WAS BORN TO THIS...BECAUSE SOMEDAY I'LL BE A GREAT WRITER AND LIVE ON THE BEACH AND WRITE FOR THREE HOURS AND DRINK GIN FOR THE REST OF THE DAY...I'LL TAKE YOUR TEN BUCKS, BUT I'D DO THIS FOR NOTHING JUST TO SEE THE AWE IN YOUR EYES...LITTLE PEOPLE, WATCH AND LEARN...AND BE HUMBLE FOR THE FIRST TIME IN YOUR ARROGANT LIVES...And Eddie Mitchell, St. Vincent Ferrer's most famous (and only) alleged Communist, chug-a-lugged the pint of gin. He only needed one breath. And when he finished, he smiled contemptuously and wiped his mouth with the back of his hand just as Robert Mitchum would have done. And smiled his condescending smile. For Eddie Mitchell that was flamboyant.

EB laughed with appreciation and hugged him. He had to admit it, alleged Communists were interesting people.

He loved Eddie Mitchell.

The boys paid him off. And they all went back into the bar. EB watched Mitch closely for the next hour or so, but he remained clear-eyed. He even sipped a beer or two and seemed to show no ill effects. About 1AM, they left Campbell's and McQuire's and made their way to Osgood's. They were in a group of seven or eight, and Mitch was with them. They entered Osgood's, and Mitch was with them. He was with them.

Then he was gone.

Nobody worried about him. At last look, he seemed fine. He probably went to get something to eat. Good idea.

144

Somewhere around 2AM, EB started feeling his beer and, as was his style when he felt that way, he simply, quietly slipped out of the saloon and started for home. His friends knew that's what he did when he had enough beer. So his sudden disappearance didn't alarm anyone either.

One of the many great things about living in Brooklyn in the Golden Age was that you didn't need a car. Of course, even if you did need a car, you couldn't have one anyway. But the point was that in Brooklyn there would never be such a thing as drunken driving for EB and his friends.

Drunken driving then was not a factor.

Drunken walking, on the other hand, was standard operating procedure.

And the beautiful thing was that you could still walk anywhere in that neighborhood at 2AM and not give it a thought.

EB walked along Nostrand to Glenwood Road and took a left. It had started to snow about an hour before. A light, dry, fine, "laying" snow that covered everything, even the sidewalks and streets, immediately. There were about two inches on the ground as EB walked along. He wasn't drunk, but he was close. His head was down, hanging, and as he reached Brooklyn Avenue, he became aware that he was following tracks in the snow. Footprints: the only disturbance to the virgin snow. And if EB was screwed up, this guy was a basket case. The tracks were weaving from one side of the sidewalk to the other. At one point, the guy stopped and leaned against the trunk of a tree. The footprints were going forward and backward around the tree. Strange, really strange.

The tracks moved on, weaving in even larger swings. If this guy wasn't careful, he'd swing out into the street. Thank goodness there was no traffic at all. EB felt like the great Chingachgook now. He was really a Mohican now. He was actually tracking this guy. When he crossed 39th Street, the tracks changed dramatically. Now there were no foot prints; there were only round indentations and long parallel troughs that sort of slid into each other. EB stopped. What the hell was going on?

He moved on.

Now there were hand prints next to the round, sliding imprints.

Geez, the guy was crawling.

EB reached 40th Street and rounded the corner, following the tracks. This was his block...and Eddie Mitchell's block.

Oh my God, Eddie Mitchell!

He was following the tracks of his dear friend. And he was scared. What if Mitch didn't make it home?

He didn't.

EB found Eddie Mitchell sprawled out on his front lawn. So near and yet so far. He wasn't covered in snow, so he hadn't been there for very long.

But was he dead?

EB tried to rouse him. Tried to get him up. He couldn't budge the dead weight, but as he was manhandling him, Mitch was grunting, so he knew he was alive. EB again tried to lift him. Too heavy. Now what the hell was he going to do? A thing like this could sober you up in a hurry. He couldn't leave Eddie here. He really would die. EB knew he had to get the Mitchell family out of the house to help him get Eddie into the house. But if they saw him, talked to him, it would be obvious that he had been drinking. And he was only sixteen.

Mitch was almost eighteen, practically legal, so it was OK that he was passed out on his front lawn. But Mr. Mitchell, the sainted cop, would throw EB, the sinning teenager, in the slammer.

At least those were his beer-clouded thoughts on this cold, wintry morning. So he did the only thing he could do.

He rang the Mitchell's bell about nine times...and ran like hell.

He hid behind a tree in front of Overholt's house, which was diagonally across the street. And he watched. The front lights came on and one of Eddie Mitchell's younger brothers, Charlie, EB thought it was, cautiously opened the front door, looked around quickly, closed the door, shut off the lights, and presumably went back to bed.

Geezus!

Stupid kid, EB grumbled, drunkenly.

Nobody rings a bell and runs away at three o'clock in the morning, you little shithead, moaned EB.

He had to do something. So he did the manly thing. He returned to the Mitchell house and rang the bell ten times.

146

And scampered back to his hiding tree, panting hard.

The lights came on, the door opened, and again eight-year-old Charlie emerged and hesitantly looked around. But this time he screwed up his courage and descended a few steps and saw the dark form spread out on his front lawn.

He screamed.

And ran back into the house. Quickly lights lit up every floor of the house. And soon a crowd of Mitchells came pouring out the front door. It took Mr. Mitchell and three of his older sons, Richard, William, and John, to carry Eddie into the house.

Nobody even thought of looking around for the bell ringer.

The mornings after were torture for EB.

He would awake in the late morning or early afternoon. And lay there berating himself. He was becoming his father.

Could he be an alcoholic at age sixteen? What was he doing? This was bad. He was too young. He was in danger of destroying his life forever. And what of his mother? It must be hurting her. And for that matter, what about his (sober) father? They must have known how late his hours were. And what he was doing when he was out that late. But they never said anything. They never lectured him. They never rebuked him. He knew they were worried about him. But, as always, his life outside the house was a mystery to them and they hoped...assumed...he was not acting irresponsibly or stupidly. They knew he would never act criminally.

And they were right about that last one.

He thought about these things often. The thoughts tortured him often. But, like most people, he did not often follow the thoughts with action. All his friends did what he was doing, and they were his second family...his street family. And his loyalty to them and their life-style would continue.

The Code.

By the spring of 1951, they had a new saloon.

It was a neighborhood bar called Grote's. It was located on Avene H, right off Albany Avenue. That was the heart of their neighborhood. Or as close as they dared to go at that time. They considered Grote's their very own saloon.

A clubhouse.

The old-timers...the regulars...accepted them, so there was no need to take the low-profile route they were forced into at Campbell's and McQuire's and, to a lesser extent, Osgoods. No, in Grote's they could be themselves. They could let it all hang out. And they did. Which meant lots of noise, lots of political arguments, and above all...lots of singing.

Perry Como rides again!

What was it about drinking beer in Irish neighborhoods and singing songs? They seemed forever linked. Everybody who could remotely carry a tune raised their voices in showy, histrionic renditions of "Danny Boy", "Old Man River", "Tell Me Why","Here In My Heart", and "Prisoner of Love". You didn't have to be Irish to break out into song in Grote's, although it's an undeniable fact of life that a little Irish blood helped you hit the big money notes. EB, John ("Jake") Teahan, Billy Janson, were the singers of the crowd. Bobby Waegelein was passable, but Matty and Jerry Frost couldn't sing a note; neither could Jimmy Ready or Joe McGrath. (Handsome Joe to everybody who knew him. Naturally, he gave himself that very descriptive nickname.) Any one of the singers was liable to break out in song at any time, even in the middle of a conversation.

But only after 1AM, of course, when the throat was fully lubricated.

EB had reached semi-legal status. He was seventeen. Not that it mattered in Grote's where, if you were a neighborhood kid and you were old enough to shave, you were old enough to drink a beer at the bar.

The bar was U-shaped and small. As you walked in the front door, you faced the bottom of the "U". On your right, up two steps, was the entrance to a back room that was more spacious than the bar area. It was equipped with tables and chairs. It was kind of run down; clean, but old. There was a big juke box standing in front of the back wall near the entrance to the men's room. ("Here in My Heart" by Al Martino, "I'll Walk Alone" by Don Cornell, "Anytime" by Eddie Fisher, and "Some Enchanted Evening" by the great PC.)

There was bar space for only about twenty stools and, on

a good night, the standees at the bar were three or four deep. So the back room was often used as part of the bar. Grote's was small and a little hard on the eyes, but it was comfortable and familiar. It was home. It was the quintessential "Cheers" bar where..."everybody knows your name and they're all so glad that you came."

The bartender at Grote's was a living legend by the name of Jimmy. He seemed to EB to be at least one hundred and twenty-five years old. He had a worn, deeply seamed face that was right out of central casting. He had lines on every square inch of his fascinating face. There were lines upon lines, there were lines that ran out of space and were forced to criss-cross over each other this way and that. And out of the center of those deep fissures grew the most enormous, regal, elegantly hooked nose that EB had ever seen outside a Tyrone Power pirate movie. And to complete the pirate visual, he had kind of hook for a hand.

Well, it really wasn't actually a hook, more like a shrunken stump. Whatever it was, his shriveled left hand simply stayed tight to his chest. Useless.

Jimmy the Bartender's visage was a little unsettling, his manner was gruff and so was his voice, but he was kindly to the boys. And he was easily the best bartender in Brooklyn. A pro's pro...because he bought back.

Not every fourth round like a journeyman bartender.

No.

No, Jimmy the Bartender bought back every other round. At least he did most of the time for EB and his friends. At least he did when he didn't forget. And when he did forget, the boys would remind him. And sometimes they would remind him even when he remembered.

Then he'd forget that he remembered and buy another one.

After all, when you're a hundred and twenty-five, your mind is not as sharp as it was when you were just a hundred.

And after all, they were still wiseguys.

Even to those they loved.

There were a few times on slow weekday nights in the

winter of 1951 that EB and a couple of his friends would come into Grote's and dump the entire contents of their pockets onto the bar. They would count it carefully (it was inevitably all change... pennies not excluded) and, pooling all the money, they would find to their disappointment that they had enough to buy one round. Which they would sip slowly, lovingly. And thank Jimmy the Bartender sincerely when he bought the next round.

Yes, Grote's was home.

In the world of saloons, one other thing of significance happened during the winter of 1951.

McDade's was sold.

McDade's, that sacred edifice, that temple, that pantheon of bars, was sold to two young men, one of whom was a just a mere ten years older than EB and his friends. The new name of the bar was Joyce and Flannagan's, but that didn't matter; everybody in the neighborhood would always call the bar McDade's. It was the change of ownership that would change things for the boys.

Heretofore, McDade's was off limits because it was the true neighborhood bar where their fathers and the elders of the neighborhood drank their shots and chasers. Some of the old-timers stopped in more than once a day, and a few of them did not want anybody to know they were wetting their whistles when their wives thought they were only walking the dog. So they snuck in the side door on Albany Avenue, where it was less likely that they would be seen. To the older men, McDade's was a private clubhouse. Their home away from home. Their special place. Their hiding place. And they didn't want any underage blabbermouths hanging about and compromising their security.

Therefore, young, semi-legal beer drinkers need not apply.

But it seemed that the advent of Barney Flannagan would change the equation. He was too young to really relate to the old-timers. Although he was a seasoned bartender, a part-owner, and a businessman, and knew that the old-timers were the basis of his business, he still needed someone to talk to.

Acting the stereotypical listener was one thing, but sometimes even a bartender needs someone to lend an ear.

After all, bartenders are people, too.

During the winter of 1951 and into the spring of 1952, the Korean War was at its height. Navy, Army, Marine, and Air Force uniforms were a common sight. Neighborhood boys were coming home on leave and that was a cause for welcome celebrations.

And what better place than McDade's?

Neighborhood boys were enlisting, not one by one but in groups, and that was cause for farewell celebrations.

And what better place than McDade's?

Slowly but surely, EB and all his friends moved into McDade's. They moved in like the in-laws that came for a week...and stayed for twenty years.

Suddenly one day, McDade's was their bar. And the old-timers were OK with it. And as a result of that, Barney Flannagan had people he could empathize with.

But they didn't abandon Grote's. That was a place they could take a girl. You couldn't, wouldn't, take a girl to McDade's. For many reasons, but on top of the list would be the fact that McDade's was a down and dirty saloon. With no pretensions to being anything other than a drinking hole. McDade's had no back room to speak of. And the front room was only the bar and not much else. It was a bar, period. The main entrance was on Glenwood Road. When you took two steps in from the front door, you were at the bar.

Hello!

The room, like its neighbor Pease's candy store, was a simple elongated rectangle. Looking from the door, the bar was on the left, and on the right there was space for a few small tables covered with red-checkered tablecloths before a two-foot jag narrowed the room allowing for just the bar, a jukebox against the wall, and a passageway to the rear. It was a straight bar that ran down the entire length of the room and ended at a small back room containing a few more tables and chairs.

The embossed tin ceiling and the plaster walls were both painted beige, again just like Pease's candy store. (Must have had the same interior decorator.)

Truth is, McDade's was even down-scale from Grote's.

But the essence of any saloon is not in the building, or the paint. It's in the people. And the people made McDade's a special place for EB.

17

Chapter Seventeen-Cars and Joyrides

The age of the automobile dawned suddenly for EB and his friends. In the spring of 1951, without too much advance notice (or advance planning for that matter), Jerry Frost and Jake Teahan bought a well-used car.

Well, not a car as much as a relic.

It was a 1932 Buick.

They paid fifty-five dollars for it.

And it was worth it.

The Buick was big, like a Sherman tank. It was black, of course, and inside it was cavernous. It had immense sofa seats covered in a rough, velour-like fabric. And, most fascinating to EB, it had grab handles in the rear covered in the same fabric. He thought that was the height of luxury. When you sat in the back seat, you sat up so high that you actually looked down on the front seat occupants. Strange. It was like sitting in the back seat of a movie theatre. And it felt almost as far away.

The stick shift dominated the front of the car. It stuck up about two feet from the floorboards. It was topped with a tennis ball sized round knob made of steel. Very tactile. Very purposeful. The starter button was on the floor, and when you started the car, you had to manipulate your foot so that when you pressed the starter you also pumped the gas pedal.

It was a sad old-timer, but oddly regal, and it still worked.

Neither Jerry nor Jake knew how to drive, so naturally they taught each other. It was just a matter of doing it, they maintained, and they were right. After awhile, when he could drive passably well, Jerry took EB up to Cortelyou Road, a deserted, unpaved street with deep potholes that ran alongside Holy Cross Cemetery, and tried to teach him how to drive. The lesson was hilariously inept. EB had a bit of trouble synchronizing the uptake of the clutch and the downward press of the gas pedal. So they jerked forward in fits and starts and stalled the engine. Restarted the engine and did it again. And again. And ingloriously inched and jerked their way along Cortelyou Road. It was a scene right out of Laurel and Hardy. But to his credit, Jerry Frost did not laugh and showed great patience.

After all, a few weeks before, that old pro was doing exactly the same thing.

That summer, EB, Jake Teahan, and Eddie Mitchell got jobs working for the Parks Department of the City of New York. It was the dream summer job for all of them. They worked six days a week at Riis Park...the city park at the beach. Their beach.

Perfect.

They were getting paid for being where they would have been anyway. They handed out beach umbrellas; they worked at the snack bars; they were the starters at the pitch 'n putt golf course; they manned the handball, paddle ball, and basketball courts, and when they were caught goofing off, they picked grass from the cracks of the roadbeds.

Great summer, dream summer.

When it was Jake's turn to have the Buick, he drove them to work in a style that was admittedly a little unfashionable, a little dowdy, and even a little gauche. But at least it was a style...the only style they had at the moment. So they endured the stares, the sneers, the twitters, and the laughs.

They sneered at the twitterers.

And laughed with the laughers.

The first day that Jake, the great veteran driver, took them to work, everything went well until they approached the toll booths at the Marine Park Bridge. Suddenly, Jake jammed on the brakes. Panicked. Cars (modern cars) were backing up behind them, or buzzing around them, as Jake sat there and shook his head...I CAN'T FIT IN THERE...he said, pointing at the narrow toll booth lanes...NO WORK TODAY, MEN...WE CAN'T GET THERE FROM HERE...said Jake, the driver. They laughed uproariously. He did, too, but he seriously believed the Buick would not fit in those tight little lanes. Cars (modern cars) were honking at them now, and if they stayed where they were, they were going to attract the cops very quickly. Not a fortuitous situation, because Jake hadn't yet taken the time to apply for driver's license.

Eddie Mitchell pointed out all the other cars that were going through the toll lanes without incident, but Jake was unconvinced...YEAH... BUT THEY'RE NOT DRIVING A CAR THAT'S WIDER THAN THE WHOLE DAMN BRIDGE...he insisted, as he began to lurch the Buick forward...still doubtful, but gaining some confidence. They reached the toll booth and Jake became aware of how much space he really had around him. He stopped beside the toll window, looked out the driver's side window and took an exaggerated double take...then he looked out the right side window and took an exaggerated triple take. If he ever was embarrassed, he was over it now and bound and determined, as always, to get some laughs. The toll taker, who was dressed in an ersatz police uniform, was fully aware of how the Buick had temporarily screwed up traffic and was waiting for an explanation, although he had probably already guessed the reason.

He stared at the '32 classic, then he stared at Jake...barely eighteen years old and obviously no Barney Oldfield.

Jake handed him the ten cent toll, flashed his famous toothy grin, and observed...DIDN'T YOU GUYS MAKE THESE THINGS TOO WIDE?...I COULD GET AN AIRCRAFT CARRIER

154

THROUGH HERE.
Laughter.
They all laughed. The toll taker laughed. Everybody laughed together. And they went to work at the beach.

What a great summer.
The last great summer.
For a few years.

Jimmy Ready (James Duffy Pius Ready...one of the great names of the neighborhood) joined the new automobile club when he bought a '36 Ford coupe. The one with the rumble seat. He paid thirty five-dollars for it.
And it wasn't worth it.
It was newer than the Buick, but mechanically it seemed older. It had big problems. The body was in pretty good shape, but the starter motor was an off and on kind of thing. The carburetor was cranky and the gas gauge didn't work at all. So Jimmy was constantly guessing how much gas he had left in the tank.
And guessing wrong.
Eventually they talked him into carrying an extra can of gas in the space behind the front seats. But often, too often, the Ford wouldn't start even when they knew there was plenty of gas in the tank. They ended up pushing that car up and down every street in the neighborhood. It always needed a jump start. So if you wanted to go for a ride with Jimmy Ready in his temperamental '36 Ford with the exotic rumble seat, there was a price to be paid. A price you paid, not with money, but with your arms and legs. You pushed, pushed, and pushed.
You were the starter motor.

EB was still only seventeen in the summer of 1951, but now he had access to cars...so that inclined him to want to go for rides.
Long rides.
And that inclination manifested itself at the strangest times. EB had an ongoing love affair with mountains. Mountains were the West, cowboys, horses, campfires, indians. Mountains were tracking and hunting. Mountains were John Wayne. They were majestic; they were beautiful; they were romantic...and they

were far away.

He longed to see the Rockies but he would settle for the Catskills.

One Friday night in mid-May, while drinking beer at Grote's, EB got the itch to travel, and around midnight, he started getting under the skin of the available drivers and the possible passengers. He started with a word, a suggestion, then followed that with a quiet paragraph or two, and then finally worked himself up into a diatribe. And he wouldn't shut up...THE MOUNTAINS AT DAWN...BEAUTIFUL...WOULDN'T IT BE GREAT?...WE COULD LEAVE NOW AND BE BACK BEFORE NOON...LET'S TAKE A RIDE...A FREEDOM RIDE... YEAH... CLEANSE OUR SOULS...THIS BAR STINKS, WE NEED SOME FRESH AIR...WE NEED SPACE...WE'RE IN A RUT...WE NEED TO BREAK OUT...FREEDOM...he kept it up for an hour or so, going from one target to another. But the truth is, there was little persuasion needed. Some of his targets were easy marks. Matty was always game for anything. Bobby Waegelein was a gamer, too. If there was a full moon, Billy Janson was a lock. Eddie Mitchell, that closet romantic, was a sure thing. If Frost or Stuchbury were there, they could be counted on. On this night, EB, Matty, Bobby Waegelein, and Eddie Mitchell were the passengers. The '32 Buick was the designated car, and Jake Teahan, their very own Barney Oldfield, was the designated driver.

Done.

At 3AM they left Grote's bar and headed for the Catskills. Singing all the way..."Tell Me Why", "Anytime", "I'll Walk Alone", "Because of You", "Maybe","Mona Lisa".

Crossing the George Washington Bridge was the breakout point for EB. The sight of the Palisades on the New Jersey side of the Hudson River was always thrilling for him. Even in the dark, that perching, precipitous bluff, that black Rock of Gibraltar shape was awesome. The Palisades were the beginning of the mountains for him.

Once across the bridge, they headed north on Route 9W. There was no other traffic on the road and thank goodness for that. They passed Bear Mountain in forty-five minutes. Two hours later, they were in the Catskill Mountains. Just in time to witness the sun come up over the tree-covered hills (calling the Catskills "mountains" was a local conceit).

156

It was unarguably beautiful.

And for these city kids, there really was a sense of freedom in the sight of it, the feel of it, the sound of it. The stillness of it. They were parked on an overlook. Some of them were in the car, some standing outside. Looking. Absorbing. Silent.

They stayed there until the sun was fully up and over the hills. Then they got back in the car and headed home. They continued their silence. EB was feeling a little hung over, but he was satisfied. The mountains filled him with a feeling of contentment. He didn't understand why and he didn't think it was important to try figure it out. That's just the way it was. Maybe he was a close friend of the great Chingachgook in a previous life.

He liked that explanation.

It was as good as any.

No, it was better than most.

On 9W South somewhere north of Bear Mountain, they saw a sign for Old Storm King Mountain Road. Almost in unison they shouted at Jake Teahan to take the mountain road. They were tired, a little hung over and hungry, but Old Storm King Mountain sounded too good to miss. Jake swung onto the road, which was hardly more than a trail. It was very narrow with room for only one car at a time. The road looked like it was last used when the Buick was brand new. To complicate things a little more, the road almost immediately rose at a forty-five degree angle. The '32 Buick was game, doing its best, but soon started to run out of breath, not to mention horsepower. It started strongly but faltered. Jake was downshifting like crazy, but even first gear didn't have the necessary torque. They were chugging up Old Storm King Mountain at three miles an hour and slowing...GET OUT, ALL OF YOU...WE NEED TO LIGHTEN THE LOAD...shouted Captain Jake. And the four boys opened the doors on each side of the car and, laughing all the way, abandoned ship. They jogged alongside the car for another fifty yards or so till it sputtered its last sput...and died.

Another victim of Old Storm King Mountain. EB was a little embarrassed for the proud and regal old Buick, but the others had more serious things on their minds. Like how to get back down the mountain. They couldn't turn around, so they figured they had to back the car down. That bothered Jake a little bit because he didn't know too much about going in reverse. He had just barely mastered going forward.

So the four boys agreed to stay outside the car and guide it down. Eddie Mitchell suggested that they line up across the rear bumper and basically inch the car down the mountain. Matty reminded him that the Buick weighed about nine thousand pounds (not a scientific measurement) and what if Jake lost brake power and the car ran over them all. Good point, agreed Comrade Mitchell.

So they lined up across the front bumper on the uphill end of the car, each kid holding on with all his strength. They inched (or yarded) the car down as Jake, with the car in neutral, furiously pumped the brakes and slowly steered the old Buick down Old Storm King Mountain.

They reached 9W without incident. Once on level ground, the Buick started up like the old pro it was and they drove home.

Now they had other problems.

They didn't tell anybody they were going to the mountains except the other guys in Grote's. Their parents were not telephoned, telegraphed, or otherwise informed that they would not be home that night. They just did it like they did everything else. They talked about taking off to the mountains among themselves, discussed it among themselves, and made the decision to do it by themselves, with no outsider involvement, with no outsider input. Now it was over, and on the way home they were filled with mixed emotions.

It was an adventure, it was exciting, it was thrilling.

It was also stupid, dangerous, and irresponsible.

Those were their unstated thoughts as they rode home through the streets of the city, silent, glum, with dry mouths, nagging headaches, and rumbling stomachs. It was quiet in the car. They were tired and hungry and did not feel like talking. What they did feel was a palpable sense of depression because they knew that they would now have to pay the price for their impulsiveness. Each in his own way. Or each in his own parent's way.

EB's price was small.

When he arrived home about 11AM on a beautiful Saturday morning in mid-May, his parents were at first relieved that he was safe. He was then asked to explain his overnight absence and he told the truth, as always. His mother, particularly, was upset by the combination of late hours and beer drinking.

For obvious reasons.

But she couldn't chew him out for not calling since they did not own a telephone. (A family disadvantage craftily turned into a momentary EB advantage. The other guys had no such opportunity.) So his mother chewed him out for being selfish, irresponsible, and reckless. He couldn't debate the accuracy of those charges. And he didn't.

EB's father was more casual. He'd had a tough night of his own the night before and was, understandably, a little more empathetic. He was obviously glad to see his son in one piece and let it go at that. He offered EB a very welcome breakfast of bacon and eggs and told him to get some sleep.

Comparing notes a few days later, the boys agreed that their parents acted responsibly and in perspective. Their various punishments were relatively minor, as they expected. As they had been for most of their lives. They had always been allowed to live their own lives, and now anything more than a mild rebuke and a serious, sit-down discussion of their responsibilities toward themselves, their family, their church, and their society would have been seen by the boys as out of proportion. After all, in the month of May in the year of Our Lord 1951, they were practically grown men.

All in all, they had gotten away with a dicey caper.

So naturally, they wanted to do it again.

And it wouldn't take them very long.

That first spontaneous trip to the mountains occurred before the start of their summer jobs, so there was no problem with calling in sick or missing time on the job. But after Memorial Day, some of them were working, so the logistics were a little more complicated.

One mid-week night at Grote's, Eddie Bohan started talking up the Catskills. It was early July, the week after Fourth of July. EB was off the next day, so he was the first one to encourage Eddie to start recruiting. Quickly, Matty, Ed Stuchbury, and Ed Mitchell were on board. Stuchbury wasn't working for the summer and, of course, neither was Comrade Mitchell. Matty hated his job, and so the five boys were ready to go. Eddie Bohan left the bar to borrow his uncle's car. ("Borrow" might be slightly misleading because his Uncle Larry was away on a business trip. But since Eddie had previous permission to use the car around the neighborhood, they figured "borrow" was close enough.) When Eddie returned with the car, he called for a gas pool and they dug into their pockets. Only to find that they were collectively broke. They had money for gas and that was about it. Doubts started to creep in. Should they go to the mountains without any money? What if something happened?

Naaah...nothing will happen. But what would they eat? It was 1AM and they were already getting hungry. Eddie Bohan solved that problem by promising them that his grandmother, who lived in Catskill, New York, would give them a big breakfast in the morning.

They bought that and off they went.

Eddie Bohan was a year older than EB and pretty good driver. They had confidence in him, and that freed up EB's mind to indulge in his usual mountain fantasies. As the dark shapes sped by his window, he wondered what was going on in those dark and mysterious woods. Animals on the move, but carefully, stealthily. Predator and prey. Survival...for one more night. As the dawn painted in the color and the light and shade, he imagined himself riding the hills and valleys on a sure-footed Palomino who could read his mind. Western saddle hung on a colorful Navajo blanket. Winchester slung under the saddle. Six gun on his hip. John Wayne. He wondered what this land was like four hundred years ago. Before anyone was here to see it. To spoil it. Before anyone except the Indians. Who didn't spoil it. He wished he could have been the first white man to ride a horse across it. He didn't have to be a white man for that matter. He could be Chingachgook.

They didn't wait around and admire the sunrise as they did the first time. Now they were veterans. Now the ride itself, or the idea of the ride, was the raison d'être. This time they were starving and looking ahead to the scrumptious country breakfast in Eddie Bohan's grandmother's kitchen. When they reached the town of Catskill, it was about 7AM, and Eddie had considerable trouble finding the house. Which should have given the rest of them some pause. But, finally, he found it.

It was a typical fully-detached, small, white and blue frame house sitting atop a small rise. Eddie told his friends to stay in the car while he prepared his grandmother for the sudden surprise visit of five ravenous, practically grown men. He went up the driveway to the back of the house and came out ten minutes later, got in the car, and without a word started to drive away.

That was greeted with a chorus of wails and screams.

He pulled the car over, stopped, and laughed. That he was laughing was not funny...especially after he explained. He rang the bell, he knocked on the door, he peered into the windows. Nothing. A neighbor saw him, asked him who he was and, after being convinced of the truth of his identity, told him that his grandmother was on vacation...YEP, IN WISCONSIN...VISITING HER BROTHER'S FAMILY...BEEN THERE A WEEK, STAYIN' FER ANOTHER ONE, TOO.

Nice going, Eddie.

Tight, close-knit loving family, huh Eddie?

Talk to your grandmother often, do you Eddie?

Bet she'll cry when she finds out she missed you, huh Eddie?

Nice going, Eddie.

After they punished him as much as their weakened, emaciated condition would allow, they stood around a circle and pooled their money. Or rather, pooled their change. They had enough for a cup of coffee each. Or twenty five cents apiece.

They found a coffee shop and ordered their coffee. Except for Eddie Mitchell. He ordered an ice cream cone.

They laughed at him. What a kid!

But they stopped laughing fifteen minutes later when their empty stomachs started complaining again. Then it was Eddie Mitchell's turn to laugh. And he did, with a taunting glee. EB laughed with him, delighted that Mitch was zigging when everybody else was zagging. He knew that alleged Communists were supposed to be intellectuals.

And he loved it that his good friend Eddie Mitchell was nobody's fool.

The ride home was the usual quiet, irritable, hungover,

semi-depressed trip through Purgatory. But this one was notable for a violent argument between Matty and Eddie Stuchbury, who was now driving. Matty talked him into a shortcut across the Rip Van Winkle Bridge and they got lost somewhere in Yonkers.

Stuchbury was seething over that.

Then they spent a half hour in downtown Brooklyn searching for something called Wythe Avenue, which Matty swore would get them home a half hour earlier.

Stuchbury erupted over that.

And they screamed at each other for a couple of blocks while the rest of the boys did their best to ignore them. And wondered where they got the energy to battle like that. Impressive. But too loud.

Matty and Stuchbury grew silent and sulked for five minutes or so until Stuch looked at Matty and asked him whether he should take Bedford Avenue, which was his way of saying he was sorry. And Matty answered him in the affirmative, which was his way of saying he was sorry.

And that was that.

It was after noon when EB got home, and the scene was a little less emotional this time. His father was at work and his mother was beginning to get used to these little late night adventures. She let it go with some hard looks and a mild reprimand. All the other guys had pretty much the same story when they got together that night. Without really articulating it, they understood that they were programming their parents. Interesting concept.

They took one more impromptu trip to the mountains in early September, after their jobs had ended and before the schools opened.

But there was one night in mid-August when EB almost took off to the Catskills with Billy Janson. Naturally there was a full moon, and Janson, who always got a little crazy during that moon phase, had worked himself up into an emotional snit. He had his father's car parked right outside the front door of Grote's. And to make it even more enticing, it was a 1949 Chevrolet. To EB that was a brand a new car!

Tempting.

EB let himself get talked into it, but, for once, he didn't

really have his heart in it. No, on this night he really had his heart in a rekindled romance with an old girl friend from Little Flower Parish, Geraldine Croak by name. She was with him that night in Grote's, and he preferred to be sitting next to her in the backroom of a saloon than to be sitting next to Full Moon Janson in the front seat of a speeding car. Even if it was speeding to his beloved mountains. Even if it was a '49 Chevrolet.

So finally he told Janson that he'd changed his mind and was not leaving the neighborhood. Billy did not take that well and tried mightily to talk EB back into it but failed, and in his strange, full-moon way stormed out the front door of Grote's Saloon.

Gone. But not for long.

EB and Gerry, his new/old girl friend, left Grote's Saloon not long after Janson disappeared. It was early, not yet midnight, on a beautiful, soft summer night and they were strolling slowly ("Walkin' My Baby Back Home") toward her home on East 45th Street near Avenue D. They had reached the middle of the block on Albany Avenue when a car came to a screeching halt at the curb next to them.

It was Billy Janson, and he was leaning out the window and alternately cajoling and cursing EB. Apparently he wanted this adventure badly and was aggressively questioning EB's manhood.

This must be a very powerful full moon, thought EB.

The Harvest Moon, wasn't it? It must be harvesting Billy's brains, mused EB. Janson had this manic look in his eyes and this weird, strung-out kind of demeanor, and EB thought it was better for both of them if they stayed off the roads on this night. A lot of people die during the full moon, EB told him.

Billy screamed a final curse and the car roared off.

EB knew he wouldn't go very far without company and would probably go home. He also knew Billy Janson wouldn't talk to him for a day or two and then everything would return to normal.

Funny...a full moon turned the usually stable Billy Janson into a loony. And a pretty girl under a full moon turned the usually unstable EB into a lucid, caring, responsible citizen.

People sure are interesting.

Beside Billy Janson being lit up by the moon, another

loony episode occurred that fall of 1951.

They called it the "shot heard 'round the world".

They made it sound very romantic.

To EB it was no such thing. If it was any kind of a shot, it was a shot to the heart of Brooklyn. And it was fatal.

It was the third day of October in the hated Polo Grounds when Bobby Thomson hit the home run to beat the Dodgers in a playoff for the National League pennant. EB was working after school in Vick's grocery store across the street from Pease's that afternoon. They had the radio on, and EB was stocking shelves and thought the game was a lock, especially when Branca relieved Newcombe. When Thomson, an average hitter and clearly no Ralph Kiner, hit his momentous home run, EB fell off a ladder and lay on the floor of the store and railed at the fates...THOSE DAMN GODS, THERE THEY GO AGAIN, PLAYING THEIR ANTI-PEOPLE GAMES...THEIR USUAL ANTI-EB GAMES...THEIR ANTI-BROOKLYN GAMES...It wasn't fair, it wasn't fair to Brooklyn, and it wasn't fair to the great Jackie Robinson, that quintessential Brooklyn wiseguy...THE WHOLE WORLD FORGETS WHAT ROBINSON DID...wailedEB... EVERYBODY FORGETS THAT ROBINSON SINGLE-HAND-EDLY CARRIED THE DODGERS INTO THE PLAYOFFS...he finished. And he was right. Robinson did exactly that with an unbelievable dramatic catch and an equally heroric home run in the fourteenth inning of the last game of the season against Philadelphia. Going into extra innings at Shibe Park, the score was tied 8-8. In the bottom of the twelfth inning, the Phillies had the bases loaded with two out when Eddie Waitkus smashed a line drive up the middle. A certain hit, a certain RBI, and a certain game winner. It came off his bat like a rifle shot, but as it sped over second base, not inches above the bag, a gray, blue, and black blur was hurtling through space to meet it. It was Jackie Robinson...diving, straining, stretched full-out, parallel to the infield dirt. His glove hand and arm seemed to grow six inches in length as, at the last possible second, the ball met that leather barrier...that Jackie Robinson stop sign...with a SMACK!...it was a sound that could be heard all the way up in Ebbets Field. Robinson hit the dirt hard and lay there for moments as his teammates crowded around him.

It was spectacular.

Red Smith, one of the greatest sportswriters of the Golden Age, or any other age for that matter, described it this way..."the incomparable doing the impossible."

Yes.

Pennant saved.

God, what a competitor.

And if that wasn't enough, Jackie Robinson came to the plate in the fourteenth inning and hit a home run into the left field seats.

Pennant won.

God, what a wiseguy.

SO AFTER THAT KIND OF PURE ARTISTRY...THAT ELEGANT BALLET...THAT LEGITIMATE THEATER...WE GET THE CHEAP BURLESQUE OF BOBBY THOMSON?...screamed EB...It was a cruel joke. It was dirty. It was cheap...I COULD HIT A HOME RUN DOWN THE LEFT FIELD LINE IN THAT RINKY DINK STADIUM...bitched EB, the two and a half sewer hitter.

It was truly a weird year. With more weirdness yet to come. There was one more trip to the mountains in EB's future. That would come in six months, in February of 1952.

But there was another kind of trip taking shape for EB and his friends. A longer trip. Longer in time and distance. A trip to end all trips. A trip they would all take together.

Symbolically, if not actually.

The destination would be Korea.

Symbolically, if not actually.

18 Chapter Eighteen-Enlistment

EB's cousin Matty graduated from Midwood High School in January 1952. The same month EB completed the first semester of his senior year. On January fifteenth, Matty, who had enlisted in the U. S. Navy in December, left for boot camp in Bainbridge, Maryland.

Handsome Joe McGrath left a few days later.

Ed Stuchbury and Eddie Bohan were discussing going together to the Navy's downtown Brooklyn enlistment center.

Jerry Frost and Jimmy Ready tried to enlist in the Marines in early January. They were turned down because the Marines had made their quota. So they walked down the block and joined the Navy instead. (Take that, Marines!)

A call to arms! Their country needed them, as it had

needed their older brothers and cousins and neighbors in World War II. And these kids couldn't wait. In EB's neighborhood, the country's call to duty was always heard. And always heeded. This was a generation that took its responsibilities seriously. But it was a generation that took its attitudes toward war from the movies.

War was another game of "guns", only you didn't play it on the stoops and behind the bushes of East 40th Street. You simply moved the location (the stage) to the mountains, the air spaces, and the offshore waters of an obscure peninsula called Korea.

War was a wiseguy's milieu...it was smokin', cursin', bitchin', laughin', and Neil Simon dialogue. War was hip. And a guy's thing. War was an afternoon walk in the woods with your buddies. It was camaraderie; it was loyalty; it was honor; it was bravery; it was heroism.

War was the debt a man paid to his country.

War was the way a man loved his fellow man...as long as they were on the same side.

War wasn't real and it didn't hurt.

So everybody was doing it.

All his friends were answering their country's romantic, seductive, irresistible call to duty. And, of course, EB was thinking about it. But he was the youngest and the only one who was not yet graduated from high school. The rest of the boys told EB to wait the six months until graduation.

DON'T BE A JERK...they said...YOU SHOULD FINISH HIGH SCHOOL...DON'T BE A LOSER...THE NAVY HAS NO RESPECT FOR ILLITERATES...THEY'LL MAKE YOU A COOK, OR SOMETHING.

EB knew they were right.

He knew he should wait the measly six months.

But he didn't want to.

And he wouldn't.

Wiseguys normally do not listen to advice, especially good advice.

That's why they're wiseguys.

EB's mid-term report card was deplorable.

65s covered the page. 65s spread their sad message all over the page. This kid is not serious, the numbers said. This kid is not trying. This kid is just showing up. This kid is beyond redemption. This kid is a loser...

Except.

Except for that inexplicable 95 in intermediate algebra.

It shone like a perfect diamond embedded in a block of black coal. It was a message light, a numerical semaphore signaling...what?...promise or protest?...aptitude or attitude?

Or was it an SOS?

Whatever it was, it was capricious, erratic, unsettling.

This kid is weird, the numbers said.

The 65s embarrassed EB. This was his low point. He was disappointed in himself. His eight-year 94 average in St. Vincent Ferrer nagged at him. He knew he was cheating his mind...his potential...his talent. But it was done. Now what?

Now he would use the terrible report card to convince his parents that joining the Navy was the best thing for him. The report card said he was only marking time, and, more important, it said that he needed to grow up. And the Navy would do that for him. He could always finish high school in the Navy. He would take the high school equivalency courses. He would have more time to study. He would be more mature and more motivated. He would graduate high school in the Navy. And at the same time, he would get invaluable training in radio or electronics that he could take with him into civilian life after he was discharged.

Those were the arguments he used on his parents. The whole family was sitting around the dining room table as he made his presentation. And a presentation it was. He was selling hard. And, sad to say, well.

When he finished, his mother was crying.

His sister Dorothy was crying.

His father was beaming.

His dad was a Naval World War I veteran and was proud that his only son was proposing to follow in his footsteps. He had a life-long soft spot in his heart for the Navy. Like most men, he had romanticized his time in the service, and by now, in his head, it was more myth than reality. But because of that, he was a firm supporter of his son's position.

They talked it out. His mother was afraid for him. War was a testament to man's stupidity. And this one was worse than stupid. It was a war that made no sense. What was Korea? Where was Korea? Who ever heard of the place? American boys are dying. For what? She made the arguments with intensity and conviction. But she knew her objections were falling on four deaf ears...EB's and his father's.

Dorothy couldn't imagine the next three and a half years without him. For her, EB was the glue that held the family together when their father's drinking threatened to tear it apart. She needed his big-brother presence. It was a moment charged with emotion, and it was about to be exacerbated by Dorothy's oft-told tale of how her big brother had saved her life when she was four years old. It was a story that embarrassed EB a little, but since this was all in the family, and EB was the hero, and they all knew it by heart...what the heck. His self-esteem could use a little boost. After all, a little hero worship was good therapy for a guy who was basically at the bottom of his game.

This was Dorothy's story.

Their Uncle Matt had rented a cottage at Breezy Point (the western end of the Rockaway peninsula) in the summer of 1941. He and Aunt Florence invited EB, Dorothy, and their parents to share the cottage with their family for a week in the early part of August.

It made for a pretty crowded cottage.

But it was a wonderful experience because it was a very casual and relaxed atmosphere. The cottage was only about one hundred yards from the ocean, so the kids practically lived in the water and in their bathing suits.

Except for one early evening in the middle of the week.

EB and his three cousins, Matty, Barbara, and Anne, were invited to a birthday party for one of their Breezy Point neighbors. Dorothy was not invited because she was so young, and she was not happy about it. It was about four o'clock in the afternoon and she was outside the cottage pouting and playing in the sand with her little toy shovel and bucket while the older kids dressed up in the only "good" clothes they had brought with them. EB, who had just turned seven, was dressed in a blue and white sailor suit with short sleeves, short pants, long blue socks, and brand new, shined-up black shoes. He was dressed before the other kids (naturally), got checked out by the adults, passed muster with appropriate (and predictable) admiring adjectives, and went outside to be with his little sister. He thought he could tease her into feeling better.

At first he didn't see her. She was not directly outside the cottage where she was supposed to be. Then he saw her at the water line trying to fill her little play bucket.

He started walking toward her, trying as best he could to walk on top of the sand so he wouldn't dull his fabulously shined shoes. She was unaware of his approach as she moved out into the water to make it easier to fill the bucket. She was knee-deep and not looking up as a unexpectedly large roller knocked her over.

EB was running to her as she struggled to get up and was hit with another wave. Forgotten now were fabulously shined shoes and blue and white sailor suits. His entire universe was reduced to ocean waves and his little sister.

Now she was under and being dragged out by the undertow.

EB plunged into the surf up to his upper thigh, reached her, found her arm and held on. He gathered his feet under him and reached around her with his other arm. He pulled her up close to his chest as they were hit with another roller. He kept his feet and half walked and half carried her out of the water.

She was crying, scared, and expelling mouthfuls of water in giant sobs.

But she was all right.

They stayed there on the edge of the water line for a moment or two. He brushed the wet hair from her eyes, kissed her face, and calmly told her she was fine. She stopped crying and quietly agreed. With one final big sob, she gave him a little girl hug, took his hand, and together they began to walk up the beach to the cottage.

As EB and his little sister approached, the other kids came out of the cottage, and the first thing they noticed was that he was a sorry sight. Soaked. Bedraggled. Ruined. No longer party-ready. The girls ran screaming back into the cottage and ratted on him...EB WENT SWIMMING WITH HIS CLOTHES ON...they squealed. When EB and Dorothy reached the cottage, the adults were out and waiting. Dorothy was in her bathing suit, so she

170

was innocent. But EB was in his best (and only) party clothes and was obviously guilty as sin. No trial, no jury. Guilty as charged.

His mother grabbed EB's arm and started shaking him. She would have whacked him but there were too many witnesses. His Aunt Flo was screaming at him. His father was upset with him, his uncle was questioning his sanity. They were all lecturing him at once. Gesticulating, accosting, accusing. Dorothy was still in shock and didn't...couldn't...say a word. EB's mother was shaking him so hard his brains were bouncing around in his skull and stopped working. So he wasn't saying anything either.

This went on for what seemed like twenty minutes. It was a chaotic scene; it was turmoil; it was terribly confusing. But one thing was clear in his oscillating brain...he was in for a major league punishment.

And he was about to get it when a woman approached the group. She had seen the whole thing. This little boy had saved the little girl's life. He was a hero.

Everything calmed down and the woman described the action in detail. When she was finished, all the adults, including the men, were misty-eyed, and EB's girl-cousins were hugging him. They all crowded around him, they wanted to be close to him. His mother brushed the wet hair out of his eyes. And kissed his wet face.

EB was a hero.

That was Dorothy's story.

It was all too true and she told it with emotion. She told it with gratitude. She told it with tears in her eyes. When she finished, she really broke down. She would truly miss her big brother...her personal lifeguard...the family's cornerstone. And EB would miss that role as well. Because while giving that support to his little sister, he got something back beyond her love and respect. Dorothy, and his mother, too, gave him the opportunity to feel like a man...a protective man...a responsible man...even though he was still a kid. He would miss that terribly.

But he reasoned that he would be away for only a short time and honestly believed that his country needed him more than his family did. And further, he believed his father would rise to the occasion. (He didn't, not really.) Their conversation ended, predictably, in an accepting silence.

So the decision was made.

EB would quit high school with six months to go and enlist in the U.S. Navy. The family was in agreement. The father was proud, the women were crying, and the gods were smiling. The mischievous lesser gods, that is. The capricious little gods who delight in playing dice games with earth people's lives. They were smirking and giggling as they looked down upon this little human drama and prepared to roll the dice again.

But the Big God, the God who is Himself, was watching, too. And He wasn't laughing.

So He loaded the dice for the next role.

When Ed Stuchbury and Eddie Bohan agreed upon a date to go down to the Naval enlistment office, EB insisted he would go with them. They didn't believe him. But they made it easier for him by making it Saturday morning, the second of February. He was still in school and did not want to miss any days because, for all the world knew, he was serious about school and had every intention of finishing the final semester of his senior year. His plan was to reveal his enlistment plans to Midwood High School once he had been accepted and had a firm reporting date.

Stuchbury and Bohan arranged to meet in the enlistment office, and they were both sitting in the reception room when the door opened and EB walked in. They both smiled but shook their heads in disbelief and mild disapproval...WHAT THE HELL ARE YOU DOING HERE?...GO HOME AND DO YOUR HOME-WORK...they chided like big brothers. They pretended to be scolds. He pretended not to hear them. They smiled. He smiled. He was kind of proud of himself. He showed up. They didn't think he would. But he showed. He was with them.

He was one of them.

They were called one by one to an interview in one of the inner offices. When EB's name was called, he walked into a small room painted in standard government colors. Gray. Warm gray on the ceiling and walls, cool gray in the carpeting and furniture. Seated behind a small desk was a rather young First Class Petty Officer in dress blues with the crossed quills insignia of the yeo-man rating above the three red stripes on his left arm.

He greeted EB warmly.

He kept up a friendly chatter as they went through the

paper work. EB was equally polite, interested and animated as they went through the background information. He was waiting for the big question that his older cousin, Bob Campbell, World War II veteran, and at this time a Lieutenant Commander in the Naval Reserve, had prepared him for. Finally it came...SO SON, WHAT WOULD YOU LIKE TO DO IN THE NAVY? WOULD YOU LIKE TO LOOK THROUGH THE RATINGS BOOK AND DISCUSS THE OPPORTUNITIES?...asked the oily yeoman, implying that the world was EB's, whatever he wanted, he was the boss, anything was possible, everything was doable...NO THANKS...said EB...I WANT TO BE A RADIOMAN....The young petty officer turned on his practiced smile...A RADIOMAN... GOOD CHOICE...WE NEED MORE OF THOSE...A RADIOMAN...SURE...and he wrote it in with a surety and a confidence that communicated to EB that it would happen.

Done.

AND I'D LIKE TO GO TO RADIOMAN SCHOOL IN WASHINGTON, D.C....continued EB. The yeoman looked him in the eye...WASHINGTON!...GREAT CHOICE...GREAT TOWN... GREAT SCHOOL...YOU'LL LOVE IT...as he wrote it in...WASHINGTON, D.C....SURE THING.

Done.

NOW I REALLY MEAN THIS, I KNOW YOU GUYS JUST SAY ANYTHING TO GET US TO SIGN UP, BUT I REALLY MEAN THIS...challenged EB, who straightened up in his chair and leaned aggressively toward the petty officer. It was a dramatic move. And it would have been more effective if only EB had looked older and tougher. Unfortunately for EB, on that day he looked to be no more than twelve years old...MY COUSIN WAS A GOOD RADIOMAN IN WORLD WAR II AND I KNOW I'LL BE A GOOD ONE ,TOO...the petty officer feigned taking offense at his aggression...HEY, I WOULDN'T DO THAT...TELL YOU WHAT YOU WANT TO HEAR, I MEAN...I'M HERE BECAUSE I'M GOOD AT MY JOB, TOO...AND I'M GOOD BECAUSE I TRY TO PLACE NEW RECRUITS IN THE JOBS THAT THEY HAVE AN INTEREST IN AND AN APTITUDE FOR...BECAUSE THAT'S GOOD FOR THE RECRUIT AND WHAT'S GOOD FOR THE RECRUIT IS GOOD FOR THE NAVY...YOU SEE THE TRUTH IN THAT, RIGHT?...IT JUST MAKES COMMON SENSE DOESN'T IT?...NOW YOU KNOW I

CAN'T IN ALL HONESTY GIVE YOU A GUARANTEE, BUT I PROMISE YOU I'LL DO ALL I CAN TO GIVE YOU WHAT YOU WANT...AND I HAVE A LOT OF INFLUENCE BECAUSE COMMAND KNOWS THAT I KNOW MY PEOPLE...he lied.

He lied so well that EB wanted to believe him. He wanted to, but he didn't. Bob Campbell had prepared him for that too.

In the final analysis, said Bob, they'll do what they want to do and there's no sense in making yourself nuts about it. He had learned, he told EB, that there was no right way, no wrong way, there was only the Navy way. (EB thought Bob had made that up and was very impressed.)

EB signed in triplicate and got a reporting date of Thursday, February 21, 1952.

When EB returned to the reception room, Stuchbury and Eddie Bohan were waiting for him. As they walked out of the building, they compared notes and came to the conclusion that things had gone about as well as they expected. They all made their cases for job categories (rates) but knew the chances were not good. They knew the Navy would do what it wanted to do. And while they all agreed that the young yeoman petty officer was only doing his job, they also knew he was bull-shitting them. But it didn't matter. They understood.

They were practically in the Navy now.

And they felt pretty good as they walked down Fulton Street. They walked taller. Straighter. More confident. And they wondered if anybody noticed. Then they pictured themselves walking down Fulton Street in dress blues. And they knew everybody would notice then. They felt great.

They were in the Navy now.

EB had less than a month to get his act together. The first thing he had to do was go down to the principal's office in Midwood High School and inform them that he was dropping out of school. His grade advisor was with him as they entered the principal's office. As EB went through his story, the principal made an effort to seem animated and interested and, of course, opposed to an action as rash as this...SIX MONTHS TO GO...he said...IT BORDERS ON IRRESPONSIBILITY...he chided...WAIT, FOR GOODNESS SAKE...said the principal.

EB's grade advisor supported that theme...WAIT, IT'S ONLY SIX MONTHS...SACRIFICING YOURSELF FOR YOUR COUNTRY IS A NOBLE THEME, BUT TO DO IT THIS WAY IS TOTALLY UNNECESSARY...they said practically in unison... WAIT! IT'S ONLY SIX MONTHS...actually five months, they said, as they counted the months off on their fingers...YOUR FINAL SEMESTER HAS ALREADY STARTED...WAIT!

They tried, seemingly sincerely. It was a good act. But at its heart, it had no truth. Neither one of them knew this kid. He had come to them late, only two semesters ago. Obviously he didn't want to be here, in their school. He was a terrible student (except for that enigmatic 95), so the loss to Midwood High School was minimal. Hey, it's a shame, it's foolhardy, even a little sad. But if that's what he wants, let him go.

But then the principal made an offer that EB barely paid any attention to but would prove to be a godsend.

The principal said that if EB changed his mind, or the Navy did (not understanding the Navy), he was welcome to come back to school. They would reinstate him without penalty, and if he worked hard, he could still graduate on time. A kind and generous offer that EB barely heard. But somewhere in the deep recesses of his mind, in some hidden fold or crevice, on some tenacious neuron, it stuck.

And that was a good thing.

At the end, they agreed that EB would attend school until the Winter Break, a week-long vacation that began on Monday the eighteenth of February. They also agreed to provide him with the necessary records to enable him to continue his education in the Navy. All in all, they were very nice to him. And he was vocally appreciative.

So they left on the best of terms.

And that was a good thing, too.

By now, all of EB's friends had accepted the fact that he was going. The ones who were still left in the neighborhood, that is. Matty was gone; Handsome Joe McGrath was gone. Jerry Frost and Jimmy Ready were scheduled to go just a few days before EB, Stuchbury, and Eddie Bohan. Bobby Waegelein and

Billy Janson would join the Army later that summer. But they still had time. So there were still a few guys left in the neighborhood. That was the group EB started working on for one last trip.

One last trip to the mountains.

THE CATSKILL MOUNTAINS ARE MOLEHILLS... argued EB the following Friday night in Grote's Bar and Grill ...THE CATSKILLS ARE KID-AROUND MOUNTAINS... BOGUS...PHONY...OUT THERE IN THE WEST, WHERE THE REAL MOUNTAINS ARE, THEY'D BE CALLED MOUNDS... KNOLLS...BULGES...BUMPS...HUMMOCKS...NUBS... he ranted and raved, looking serious but with eyes twinkling...WE SHOULD TAKE ONE MORE TRIP TO THE MOUNTAINS...THE REAL MOUNTAINS...NO, NOT IN COLORADO...(pause)...IN THE SHENANDOAH VALLEY OF VIRGINIA...THE GREAT BLUE RIDGE MOUNTAINS OF VIRGINIA...THE SPECTACU- LAR SHENANDOAH VALLEY OF VIRGINIA...singing now..."IN THE SHENANDOAH VALLEY OF VIRGINIA"....talk- ing now...ONE MORE TRIP BEFORE WE GO...TO REAL MOUNTAINS, THIS TIME...He was his usual pain in the ass; he wouldn't stop. They yelled at him, they threw peanuts and pret- zels at him, but they were listening.

And they were succumbing to the lure of the road.

The concept of one last adventure appealed to them. They knew they would all be gone before long. And be gone for a long time.

Bobby Waegelein was the first to sign up and said he could get his grandmother's car...a '38 Nash. (If the '32 Buick was a Sherman tank, the Nash was a Panzer.) Eddie Bohan bought in and volunteered to drive. Ed Stuchbury sighed, shook his head, rolled his eyes, and joined up. The last passenger was James Duffy Pius Ready, who volunteered for his first road adventure. That made five. Pot right. But this one would be sanctioned. They would tell their parents in advance. This one would be organized and could last for a few days. Virginia was a long way off. Therefore, they would actually stock up on food, or more accu- rately, junk food. But no beer, no drinking, they agreed. For this one, they would need maps. And planning.

And this one would be started in the daylight.

That would be different.

EB was excited. Of course, he had no idea how high the Blue Ridge Mountains really were. And he really didn't care. He just knew they were a lot higher than the puny Catskills and a lot farther away. The weather reports were good and clear, but it was the winter and the Blue Ridge were sure to be snow-covered. If they were stark enough, and using just a little imagination, they could become the Grand Tetons.

Or the Bitterroots of Lewis and Clark fame.

Whatever they turned out to be, the idea of them was intoxicating.

The storied Shenandoah Valley...it sounded wonderful.

The last trip.

He couldn't wait.

19 Chapter Nineteen-The Last Trip

They shoved off (Navy talk) at 6AM on Tuesday, February 12th. The weather was clear and cold. There had been no snow storms in the previous month, so the roads were dry.

The trunk of the car was well stocked with food...potato chips, pretzels, Cheese Doodles, two cans of Campbell's (no relation) Pork 'n Beans, Hershey bars, Cokes, and one package of Slim Jim's (for Eddie Bohan, the only person EB ever knew who could eat, no less savor, the vile tasting Slim Jim's). Otherwise they traveled light. They had no change of clothes, no shaving kits, no soap, no extra underwear, no extra shirts, no extra sweaters...no extra anything.

The plan was to reach the Shenandoah Valley by mid-afternoon, take in the mountains, sleep in the car, and leave for home in the morning. So there was no need, no space, no time for the niceties.

They were on the trail.

Hygiene was out, grunge was in.

This was man's work.

The effete need not apply.

The five boys took up all the space there was in the interior of the car. Eddie Bohan was driving, Bobby Waegelein was awarded the front passenger seat because it was his grandmother's car. That was only fair. EB, Stuchbury, and Jimmy Ready were in the rear. It was tight, but they were in an up-beat mood, excited, exhilarated. They were happy to be on the road again, particularly when the destination was the fabled Blue Ridge Mountains and the Shenandoah Valley as described (and romanticized) so vividly, and so often, by the ever-garrulous EB.

They followed the New Jersey Turnpike to the Memorial Bridge, and from there followed Route 40 into Baltimore, where they picked up Route 1 into Washington DC. Anything south of Delaware was a new experience for all of them. They grimaced at the row houses of Baltimore and gawked at the beautiful, open, rolling hills of Maryland. South of Washington DC, at Arlington, they swung west on Route 211. They followed that to Route 11, where they again headed south...straight down the Shenandoah Valley. They made it. But it did not take them nine or ten hours as they were told. It took them over fourteen.

So they didn't make it by mid-afternoon.

They made it by mid-evening.

And it was dark.

And the beautiful, fabled Shenandoah Valley was not to be seen. It was invisible.

Slight miscalculation.

But what the hell, it was a great ride down. (Any ride was a great ride.) And they would see everything in the morning. Right now, though, their problem was the night. They needed to find a place to sleep. No, not a hotel or motel.

They already had lodging...they were riding in it.

They needed a place to park. A place where they would not be disturbed by cruising police cars. Kids from Brooklyn were wary of southern cops. They had heard the stories and saw no reason to test the truth of them. Eddie Bohan continued to drive south looking for a quiet, out of the way place to park for the night. Eddie pulled off the highway at a little town called Staunton. They remember it well because the road signs proclaimed it as the "birthplace of Woodrow Wilson" and, judging by the quantity and the quality of the signs, the locals seemed damned proud of it.

OK! EB and his friends could understand having pride in your hometown, so they decided to spend the night in Staunton.

Eddie found a small parking lot near a railroad station, and that's where he parked. He figured they wouldn't attract any attention in a parking lot even though there were only two other cars in the lot. Hey, it was a small town. It was after 11PM, and they bedded down for the night...so to speak. EB could never sleep in a car. He could never sleep sitting up. And besides that, it was cold. They were dressed warmly and they had blankets, but it was uncomfortable as hell. He was miserable. He wondered why he put himself through this kind of agony. He fussed. He squirmed. He sighed dramatically. Stuchbury told him to shut up. Jimmy Ready mumbled bad things under his breath. EB tried to settle down. He even dozed for an hour or so, woke up, dozed for another hour, woke up and then stayed wide awake. He stayed that way for another hour then he couldn't stand it any longer, so he opened the door and walked around the car. He was pissed off at himself and cold and hungry, too. Why did he do stuff like this? Why didn't they plan this in advance and arrange for a cheap hotel or something? Nobody can sleep in a car. It's inhuman. Of course he knew very well why they were not staying in a hotel. The problem was a familiar one. It was called money. They needed it. And they didn't have it.

At least they had agreed to splurge on a hot breakfast in the morning. That was something to live for.

It was quiet, not a soul in sight. EB looked over at the railroad and saw a tiny building. A shack, really. There was smoke coming out of a flimsy looking pipe chimney that was struggling to stay attached to the roof.

Mmmmm, thought EB. Fire. Heat. Cooking.

He knew Jimmy Ready's mom had made him take two cans of Campbell's Pork 'n Beans. And EB began to salivate. But they were Jimmy's beans. Small problem.

EB returned to the car, opened the door, and sidled in next

180

to Jimmy. He whispered in his ear...I KNOW YOU'RE NOT SLEEPING...C'MON LOOK AT ME, YOU MISERABLE BASTARD...YOU'RE COLD AND SUFFERING AND STIFF AND VERY HUNGRY...AND I AM HERE TO HELP...Jimmy opened his eyes, smiled that little sarcastic smile of his and said...GET THE HELL AWAY FROM ME...IF I'M MISERABLE IT'S BECAUSE OF YOU...that didn't stop EB. Didn't even slow him down...JIMMY, ARE YOU HUNGRY?...No answer...JIMMY, ARE YOU HUNGRY?...mmm, mumble...JIMMY, GET YOUR TWO CANS OF BEANS OUT OF THE TRUNK AND I'LL SHOW YOU HOW TO COOK 'EM...C'MON, GET UP...LET THESE OTHER SHITHEADS SLEEP...WE'LL HAVE A FEAST...C'MON, GET UP...I'M GONNA GET YOU WARM...YOUR SALVATION IS AT HAND.

Jimmy Ready threw off his blanket. They got the beans from the trunk and walked over to the shack. They opened the door cautiously, hoping the shack would be empty at two o'clock in the morning.

It wasn't.

The shack was small, maybe fifteen feet square, and very spartan. It was warm and dark. A dim and bare 40 watt light bulb hung down over the entrance. The only other light source was the glow from the pot-bellied stove that stood in the center of the room. Arranged in a semicircle in front of the stove were four simple wooden chairs. They were all empty except one. The fourth chair was a rocking chair occupied by an old black man who instantly reminded EB of Walt Disney's Uncle Remus. To the two boys he looked a little frightening as he rocked in and out of the shadows. His skin was very black and his hair was very white. He had an engineer's striped hat sitting on his enormous, impressive white head, and he was dressed in layers of clothing that seemed to go on and on. He was smoking an old pipe that looked handmade. EB and Jimmy hesitated, unsure of themselves. Was this old-timer a railroad worker or was he a railroad bum? EB thought of all those depression movies he had seen with the bums riding the rails and the railroad dicks searching them out and throwing them off the trains and not waiting for a stop, either.

With a wave of a double-gloved hand, the old-timer invited them in.

They sat on the wooden chairs, jacket pockets bulging with cans of Campbell's Pork 'n Beans. And they talked. Or rather the old-timer asked questions: where they were from; where they were going; what they were doing here; what they were doing for the rest of their lives? They answered him honestly. They didn't run any scams on this rather mysterious old-timer. In truth, they were a little intimidated. They didn't know a lot about black men, and they paid him the respect due him as the one whose turf they were invading.

That was their way, no matter where they were.

So they talked and grew more comfortable in his presence. They brought up the subject of using the stove (his stove?) to cook their beans. He allowed as to how that was fine with him. Jimmy opened the two cans with an opener his mom had thoughtfully included in his little care package, and the boys put the two cans of beans on the top of the stove, sat back in their chairs, and continued to shoot the breeze with the Uncle Remus look-alike. During the next fifteen minutes, Uncle Remus never mentioned the beans, but the boys could scarcely get their eyes and their minds off them. And as they talked, their eyes darted back and forth from the beans to the old-timer.

Pretty soon the beans started bubbling and so did the boys. They couldn't wait to wrap their tongues around those warm beans, dripping with delicious pork-infused juice. At last. Feasting time was here. But, should they offer their new friend some beans? They looked at each other, uncertain.

YOU BOYS ARE NOT GONNA EAT THAT, NOW ARE YA?...said Uncle Remus...NOT OUTTA THOSE THERE CANS...YOU BOYS ARE NOT THINKIN' OF DOIN' THAT, ARE YA?...YOU BOYS EVER HEAR OF PTOMAINE POISONIN'?...EB and Jimmy stopped, frozen. What the hell was this old guy talking about? Ptomaine poisoning? What the hell was ptomaine poisoining?

YUP...THE TIN IN THAT THERE CAN WILL LEACH INTO THE STUFF INSIDE WHEN IT REACHES A REAL HIGH TEMPERATURE...TIN WILL HURT YA, BOYS...TIN CAN KILL YA, BOYS...NEVER EAT STRAIGHT OUTTA THOSE TIN CANS, BOYS...YOU SHOULD KNOW THAT STUFF...WHAT THEY TEACHIN' YOU BOYS IN THOSE SCHOOLS UP NORTH?...EB and Jimmy still did not move. They were mesmerized. This old guy either just saved their lives or scammed them out of a hot meal.

And they weren't sure which.

I KNOW WHATCHA THINKIN'...said kindly old Uncle Remus...I DON'T WANTCHA BEANS, BOYS...HONEST...TAKE 'EM OUT OF HERE IF YA WANT, YOU DON'T HAVE TO LEAVE 'EM...BUT BE CAREFUL.... THEY'RE POISONED...AND THEY'RE REAL HOT...DON'TCHA BURN YER HANDS...

Naturally, EB and Jimmy Ready left the cans of beans on the stove. As they walked back to the car, Jimmy turned to EB and asked...WE JUST GOT SCAMMED, RIGHT?...EB smiled at Jimmy and said...ABSOLUTELY...AND IT WAS A PLEASURE.

There were only a couple of hours till dawn, and EB and Jimmy slipped quietly back into the car and tried to sleep. They tried not to disturb the others, but Eddie Bohan was awake and without even turning around asked in a whisper...WHERE WERE YOU GUYS?...NOWHERE...said EB...WHAT DID YOU DO?... asked Eddie...NOTHIN'...said Jimmy...ANYTHING HAPPEN?... pursued Eddie...NOPE...said EB.

Then they dozed for an hour or so.

At dawn they were all awake.

They found a coffee shop in town and had a nice breakfast, their first and last real meal of the day. During the meal they discussed the travel plans for the day. The waitress told them that if they followed Route 254 east for a few miles they could pick up the Skyline Drive going north. And that road would give them the most spectacular views of the valley and the mountains. It was good advice and they followed it.

It turned out that the Blue Ridge Mountains were not much higher than the puny Catskills, but the Shenandoah Valley was everything they expected. And the valley made the mountains seem higher and more dramatic. It wasn't the Rockies, but from the Skyline Drive the whole scene was indeed spectacular. So EB was satisfied.

The way north on the Skyline Drive was arduous. It was a tough drive for Eddie Bohan. The road was narrow and winding. The views were wonderful, but the going was slow. They drove all day with only one pit stop for gas. The weather was holding clear and cold.

They reached northern New Jersey around ten o'clock that night. There was no Verrazano Bridge in 1952, so they drove to the Staten Island Ferry slip and waited for the next boat.

The car was quiet. The day was long and tiring. EB was now in the front seat acting as Eddie's navigator. When they drove the car onto the ferry and parked it, nobody got out. They all fell sound asleep. Including EB and Eddie Bohan. Sound asleep.

When the ferry docked on the Brooklyn side, the cars around them had to beep and honk the boys awake. And they were not kind about it. As they drove off the boat, EB was still drowsy. But he was worried about Eddie Bohan and promised him that as his loyal navigator he would not sleep. They only had a few miles to go, and as they pulled onto the Belt Parkway eastbound and moved past the big expensive houses on Shore Road and headed toward Coney Island, EB promised Eddie that he would keep him awake.

And promptly fell asleep.

A sharp bump awakened him. In a sleep fog, he looked up and saw to his horror that the big Nash had jumped the curb and gone off the road. He screamed...WAKE UP EDDIE!...EDDI-IEEE!...as the passenger side (EB's side) of the car scraped and crunched and sparked along a four-foot high brick retaining wall that ran parallel to the road just a few feet in from the curb they had just jumped. The wall preceded an overpass, and EB thought for sure they would jump the wall and plunge fifty feet to the street below.

The car was screaming in protest and so was EB when he saw that they were about to crash headfirst into a three-foot wide abutment that was at a ninety-degree angle from the wall they were now grinding along.

EDDIIEEEE!

They hit it full force and straight on.

WHOMP...the first sound of impact was eerie...it wasn't metallic...it was a loud but low-noted...WHOMP...but that unexpected sound was instantly followed by a shrieking cacophony of crumpling, creasing, grinding, metal car parts...SCREECH...SCRAPE...GRIND...RUPTURE...SPLIT...SCRUNCH...

The right front of the big Nash crumpled and collapsed in weird shapes and directions. That elegant long hood seemed to rush back at him. EB instinctively had his arms fully extended on the dashboard to protect his face from the windshield. When the Nash hit the abutment, it first started to grind and crawl up the wall, then it stopped and slowly, pathetically, keeled over on its side.

And then the engine burst into flames.

To EB, the most amazing things were the sounds and how it all happened in slow motion. It was like watching a slowed down movie. Looking at it was fascinating. Listening to it was frightening. But living it was sickening. Surely this was happening to someone else.

No, sorry.

The Nash was now lying on its side, sadly battered and broken but still strangely stately, like a listing aircraft carrier...the Wasp...the Hornet...going down but a proud and elegant lady to the end.

And it was still burning.

Confusion. Claustrophobia. Terror. Hysteria.

Each kid was going through his own personal version of panic. EB's face was OK, it did not go through the windshield, it didn't touch the windshield. How he avoided that fate was, and still is, a mystery. He was lying on top of Eddie Bohan, who was moaning. EB was dimly aware of the general chaos inside the upended car, but it was all a haze. There was a confusion of sound, none of it distinct. EB was not aware of any pain, so he thanked God for that miracle. But he had no time to dwell on miracles past...the miracle of the future was his immediate concern. He had to get the hell out of there. As quickly as possible.

At this point, Ed Stuchbury took charge. He stepped up and became the hero. While the rest of them were still incoherent and unjumbling and untangling themselves from each other, Stuch stood up and somehow swung open one of the doors. Then he started lifting and throwing the other boys up and out of the car. In turn, each of them scrambled out on top of the wreck and either just rolled off onto the road or crouched and jumped.

EB was one of the last to go, and Stuch just basically picked him up and threw him out. EB rolled over the side of the car and hit the road on his feet.

And that was the first time he felt any pain at all.

Suddenly his right leg was killing him.

He limped to the center median where the others had gathered. They were all shouting for Stuchbury to get the hell out of there. They expected the gas tank to explode any second.

Stuchbury helped Eddie Bohan up onto the top of the car and followed him immediately. They tumbled out onto the road together. And joined the others on the median.

It was freezing. The wind had picked up during the day, and it was blowing at them with a cruel insistence as they stood there and watched the elegant old Nash burn and die.

Amazingly, there was no other traffic on the Belt Parkway, one of the busiest highways in Brooklyn. But this was 1952, and it was also close to midnight on a weekday night. They saw then that the fire was starting to diminish and they lost their fear of an explosion. Then they took stock of themselves.

They agreed that the 1938 Nash-Panzer had saved them. If the car had been built later than 1950, they figured they would all be dead.

Eddie Bohan was bleeding from the face. He had a big horizontal welt across the bridge of his nose where he had hit the steering wheel. He complained that it was broken, and they agreed that it probably was.

Everybody else was OK.

Except EB, who was now sitting on the cold concrete of the median. He felt intense pain and was probably in shock. He pointed to his leg and grimaced like crazy. Stuchbury, resuming his hero role, lifted up EB's pant leg to see what he could do.

To Stuch, EB's ankle looked like a tennis ball.

To EB, it felt like a basketball.

It was broken for sure. And he was sweating and freezing at same time.

Bobby Waegelein told EB later that the front wheel and tire on the passenger side was forced back into the cabin and up through the floorboards by the force of the crash, obviously breaking EB's ankle.

But on that night, EB didn't care how it happened; he only cared that it hurt like hell. And he was asking the others what they were going to do to get him some help.

186

Then the cops showed up.

First one patrol car arrived. Followed quickly by a second. Then a third.

It's true, bad news travels quickly.

And these cops were not very friendly. The word "punks" was thrown around, along with "jerks" and "shitheads". They realized EB was hurt so they went easy on him, but the four other boys were frisked and roughed up in the process. Not much – just a little shove here, a little push there. When the cops heard that falling asleep was the reason for the crash, they searched the car for beer or booze and perhaps drugs, although in 1952, drugs were not that prevalent among the youth of Brooklyn. Finding nothing but a half-empty bag of Cheeze Doodles, they decided to get out of the cold and they herded the boys into two patrol cars and took off for the precinct house.

At the precinct, they sat EB in a chair with his broken right foot elevated on a desk top. And questioned him pretty good...WHO ARE YOU?...WHY WERE YOU ON THE ROAD AT THIS TIME OF NIGHT?...WHERE WERE YOU GOING?... WHERE WERE YOU COMING FROM?...WHY WERE YOU THERE?...HOW LONG WERE YOU THERE?...WHAT DID YOU DO THERE?...

And, of course, he told the truth as he always did.

They all told the truth.

And that's what saved them.

The cops isolated the four other boys from each other and questioned them one by one. They were rough and threatening but not physically violent. Only when they got the same story from each one of them did the cops ease off. The story was so far-fetched, so dumb, so innocent, that it had to be true and the cops softened, coming quickly to the conclusion that these were basically good kids. A little weird, but basically their kind of kid. After that decision, they were downright kind to EB. They worried after him like a bunch of fathers or big brothers (which of course, most of them were). When the ambulance crew arrived, the cops helped place EB onto the stretcher and walked him out to the waiting vehicle with the whirling red and white lights.

And almost immediately, EB was a relatively comfortable passenger in a major league ambulance roaring through the streets of Sheepshead Bay on his way to Coney Island Hospital.

Strapped down on the stretcher, EB's head was filled with a confused jumble of thoughts...his parents, his ankle, his sister, his ankle, the Navy, his ankle, Midwood High School, his ankle, and finally, as they sped through the dark streets with the siren blasting, he thought to himself that he had never been in an ambulance in his life...but he had seen this movie before.

EB had never been in a hospital either.

And he found it a little strange but not unpleasant.

The first thing they did when they got him into the hospital was to take all his clothes. Then they covered him with a sheet (except his right leg, which they left sticking out) and wheeled him into an examining room of sorts. He was alone for only a short time, and then he was surrounded by half a dozen people... interns, attendants, nurses...who took off the sheet.

And he was laying there stark naked.

And they were all staring at him.

Not only at his leg, at him.

Embarrassing.

One of the nurses was a young black girl, and even though he was in deep shock, he couldn't help noticing that she was very pretty.

And that embarrassed him even more.

He wanted to scream at them that it was his ankle that was hurt not his whole body, and especially not his genitals, but he didn't.

It stayed strange for a moment or two, but then a young doctor entered the room and, taking pity on him, swung the sheet back over most of his body and began examining his ankle as he asked EB how it happened. He listened to the story of the car crash, and when EB finished, he announced that the ankle was broken. But it was a simple fracture, said the doctor. No big problem.

Easy for him to say.

He wasn't going into the Navy in a week.

NO...AND NEITHER ARE YOU...he said, when EB told him about the approaching reporting date...YOU'RE NOT GOING ANYWHERE FOR ABOUT SIX WEEKS...said the young doctor...AFTER SIX WEEKS YOU CAN GO ANYWHERE YOU

WANT, BUT UNTIL THEN, YOU'LL BE ON CRUTCHES... continued the young doctor...CRUTCHES!...bitched EB...I CAN'T BE ON CRUTCHES FOR SIX WEEKS!...he whined...I'VE GOT PLACES TO GO, THINGS TO DO...I'VE GOT TO GO DOWN- TOWN AND TELL THE NAVY I'M NOT GONNA BE THERE...OR I'LL BE A DESERTER...THEY'LL COME AFTER ME...THEY'LL SHOOT ME...OR HANG ME...they were all laughing. Feisty little kid, they smiled...OK, WE'LL PUT ON A WALKING CAST SO YOU CAN HAVE MORE MOBILITY...WE DON'T WANT ANY DESERTERS IN THIS HOSPITAL.

And that's what they did.

EB was held in the hospital for a week. A week! For a bro- ken ankle! Well, it was 1952, and that's the way it was.

His mother and father and sister and aunt and uncle were visiters on the first morning, driven to the hospital by Uncle Matt. EB's mother described the fear she felt when the bell rang at 2AM and she saw a police officer at the door. She thought EB was dead, she said. She almost had a heart attack, she said. Of course she was relieved that it was "only" a broken ankle, but if he con- tinued to act like a numbskull, then she would kill him herself.

Everybody laughed. She said it with a smile, but there was something about the way she said it. EB got the message. He was hurting himself, he was hurting his family, and it had to stop.

His father, on the other hand, was suddenly the take- charge guy. He was wonderful. He took care of everything. He went down to the Naval recruiting office and explained the situ- ation. They told him to bring EB back for a medical test when his ankle was healed. If he passes it, they said, they would give him a new reporting date.

His father visited the principal at Midwood High School and received a promise that they would take his son back and, if he worked hard, they would graduate him in June. So everything seemed to be working out.

Thank you, God.

And thank you, Guardian Angel.

He was disappointed that he was not going into the Navy with his friends, but he could now see clearly how irresponsible was his decision to quit school so close to graduation. Beyond irresponsible, it was dumb. And selfish. Yes, he could see that now. But now he had a reprieve.

God, I owe you one, he thought.
Thanks for giving me a break.
Pun intended.

EB enjoyed his week in Coney Island Hospital. It was not an unpleasant place to be, especially in his ward where the injuries were not that serious. They put him in a bed that was situated on a kind of porch, a glass-enclosed extension of the building that overlooked Ocean Parkway and contained only four beds. To EB, it was like a private room. There were two boys about his own age with broken arms occupying two of the other three beds. The fourth was empty. They enjoyed each other's company. They played cards, talked about all kinds of things (mostly the nurses), and listened to the radio.

And when EB's friends came up to visit, they were able to stay a little longer because the room was so out of the way. Eddie Bohan and Bobby Waegelein came up the first day and told him the Nash was unsalvageable. A total wreck. EB shook his head in wonder. They all looked at each other and were amazed that they were able to look at anything, see anything, or wonder at anything. They should have been dead.

But here they were with only a broken ankle and a broken nose to complain about. And they were not complaining.

EB and the young black nurse quickly became good friends. She was talkative, warm, and giving, with a lively sense of humor and a healthy disrespect for the rules, which endeared her to EB. The first morning when she woke him up to take a blood sample, she slipped him two packs of cigarettes, which he had asked her for the previous night when she wheeled him to his bed. She was kind and solicitous, laughing all the way. She let him sleep later in the morning, she smuggled him extra ice cream, she gave him extra food when she could manage it, she brought him tea in the afternoon. But no matter how much he begged, cajoled, whined and promised, she would not give him a sponge bath.

The ladies' man strikes out again.

190

On Wednesday, February 20th, EB's Uncle Matt came to the hospital and took him home. He gave EB an old pair of crutches he found in the basement and together they fitted them to EB's body by moving the hand holds. He had started walking on the cast in the hospital. At first, it hurt a lot. Then, after a day or two, it hurt just a little. But at the end of the week, he was using the walking cast pretty well. He wanted to use the crutches as little as possible.

By the next Monday, he was back in Midwood.

20 Chapter Twenty-Back To Midwood

There were reasons that the '40s and '50s were character building. You were expected to be on your own. No pampering allowed.

And no complaining, please.

EB was expected to be at Midwood High School every morning at 8:15AM. And he was expected to take the Glenwood Road bus to get there. Cast and crutches notwithstanding.

No car rides to the front door for EB.

Getting on the bus with crutches was awkward, but the bus drivers were nice about it and so were the other passengers. The drivers waited patiently (patience was a seldom-seen virtue among Brooklyn bus drivers) and the passengers offered to help as EB struggled up the steep steps of the front of the bus. He was proud of his athleticism and politely refused all offers of aid, but he appreciated it nevertheless. Getting off the bus was a little trickier (why was coming down always harder than going up?), but he basically bounced down the steps on one leg, landed in the street, and applied the crutches for balance. A ballet move worthy of the great Gene Kelly.

As befitting a senior senior, he had a light schedule. And it was a good thing, since carrying books from home to school and back again was out of the question. What little homework he had he did in home room or in gym class (mandatory, even for a kid with a broken leg). That last semester, he had English literature, French, social studies, earth science, and music classes. The music room was sort of isolated on the third floor of the school and arguably difficult to get to for a guy with a cumbersome cast. So EB thought he would run a scam on the young music teacher. She was just a few years older than he, relatively new to teaching, and very pretty, and on their first meeting, EB fancied that she fancied him a little and felt sorry for him to boot.

The perfect mark for a wiseguy.

EB had a long talk with her the first time he visited the music room. He whined about how hard it was for him to get around on his badly broken leg, purred to her about the Navy, how he was practically a veteran and how embarrassing it would be for him to attend a class filled mostly with freshman. She actually listened sympathetically and empathetically and said she'd make a deal with him. He would not have to attend class at all if he would commit to writing a 1,000 word essay to be submitted at the end of the term. The specific subject was up to him as long as it was about music.

He was amazed.

He usually approached these little scam jobs with a twinkle in his eye and an expectation that they would never work.

But this young music teacher bought it.

Amazing.

He left the music room feeling full of himself.

And promptly forgot his commitment to the essay.

Mistake.

The month of March passed uneventfully for EB. He was comfortable with his walking cast now and used the crutches as little as possible. But he still took them to school, partly for use, partly for propaganda. He knew he was making points with his teachers for his dogged, can-do attitude. He was never late for school, he was never late for any class, he never asked or expected any special treatment, and they admired that. He'd take the points any way he could get them because he continued to coast academically. He was showing up, but in body only. His spirit was still elsewhere. He had three months to go and he marked off the days like a convict awaiting parole.

Matty and Handsome Joe McGrath and other guys were starting to come home for their boot camp fourteen-day "leaves". That meant celebration. That meant drinking beer in McDade's. And these boot camp graduates didn't have jobs or schools to go to in the mornings, so they didn't wait for Friday or Saturday nights to do their celebrating. They partied any time they felt like it and expected EB to be there with them. That meant late mid-week nights for EB.

After one such night when he got home around 2AM, wobbling down East 40th Street on his well-worn walking cast and carrying his crutches tucked under his arm, he had a tough time getting up for school the next morning. But get up he did, like the trooper he was. Early in the morning in earth science, his first class after home room, he had occasion to approach the desk of the teacher. When EB got close to him, he reacted with an exaggerated physical withdrawal...PHEW! WHAT WERE YOU DRINKING LAST NIGHT? YOU STINK TO HIGH HEAVEN.

Embarrassing.

Lost some points there.

But it was OK, earth science was a softball course anyway.

By the beginning of April, EB had worn down the plaster "walker" they had fashioned on the bottom of his cast. In fact, he had worn through the cast itself and there was a hole in the bottom through which he could see his foot. When he returned to Coney Island Hospital on April third to have the cast removed, the young intern laughed hard when he saw it. But when he sawed it off, EB was not laughing. The intern used what could have been a torture device left over from the Spanish Inquisition. It was a small, hand-held saw that cut the hell out of EB's instep and shin as the cast was split from the foot to the knee. When the intern pulled the cast off, EB was appalled at the sight of his leg. It was bleeding down the middle from top to bottom, but that wasn't it. His leg was so atrophied that it looked like a chicken's leg. It had no muscle; it had no form; it had no shape. It was ashen, gray, and sickly white. It had little ribbons of skin hanging off it and looked dead.

He had a cadaver for a leg.

He was afraid to stand on it, but the intern insisted on it. So he did. And he was astonished when that dead stick-like stump held his weight. The intern, who was having a great time listening to EB bitch about his lost leg, promised him that the leg would resume its natural color in an hour or so and that it would regain its muscle tone with a little exercise. Exercise, he told EB. Exercise.

And that's what he did.

His Uncle Matt had driven him to the hospital in his 1951 Oldsmobile (the one Matt proudly insisted had a "Cadillac" engine), and he brought the crutches with him. When he returned home, he vowed to use them as little as possible over the next week or so and then not at all.

One of the neighbors had loaned him a sturdy old oak cane and he started walking on his recovering leg immediately. He walked around the block that afternoon and every early morning and late afternoon for a week. He used the crutches for school only for the first week. After that, he put the crutches in the cellar and never looked at them again. He took the cane to school and he doubled the afternoon walking time for another week. At the end of the two weeks, he even tried jogging on it and it was fine. Then he walked and jogged early in the morning and late in the afternoon for another week.

He was almost ready.

He called the Navy to make an appointment for the physical test. They told him to come in on Thursday, May 15th. That gave him another three and a half weeks to get stronger.

He used it well.

Every day when school ended, he started walking back to Pease's with Jack Noonan. They did that every day, weather permitting. EB figured that was about a mile. He started walking to school in the morning, too.

Another mile.

He wasn't playing basketball yet, but he was ready for the Navy.

When he walked into the Naval recruiting office, he didn't know what to expect. Would there be a team of doctors? A battery of tests? Would they conduct these vigorous tests here or would he have to go to special lab or something? Maybe a gym? Maybe they'd send him down to Bethesda Naval Hospital in Maryland? Or the Mayo clinic, perhaps? What would they do?

They directed EB into the same small, gray room that the first class petty officer had used to interview him in February. And there he was...the same young yeoman petty officer, smiling his personnel person's smile. He greeted EB as if he had known him for years. There was another older man standing in back of the petty officer's chair. He wore the uniform of an officer. EB assumed he was a doctor.

The older man asked him which ankle he had fractured...THE RIGHT...said EB...CAN YOU JUMP UP AND DOWN ON IT?...asked the officer doctor...SURE...replied EB. And he started jumping on his right leg. Up and down, up and down, up and down, maybe a dozen times...GREAT... said the officer doctor...YOU'RE FINE...and he left the room.

The young petty officer, smiling his professional smile, gave EB a reporting date of June 26, 1952.

And EB left.

Done.

Every year near the end of May, St. Augustine High School sponsored a boat ride to Playland in Rye Beach, New York (Westchester County). The boat was usually shared with Catherine McAuley High School, an all-girls school that was located on Foster Avenue and 37th Street. All the boys in St. Augustine were enthusiastic supporters of the boat ride. Not because they got to share a boat with a girl's school (though it must be said that the presence of the McAuley girls was not insignificant), but because Rye Beach was a fun place to be and the boat ride itself was very pleasant break with routine. Add the observation that final exams were imminent, and it was understandable that not many kids missed the boat ride.

EB looked forward to it every year when he was an Augustine student. Now that he was an alumni of sorts and about to enter the Navy, it suddenly became important to him that he go on one more St. Augustine boat ride. Chalk it up to nostalgia; but whatever it was, it was a strong emotion. So he asked his friend Red Wallace to get him a ticket.

It was a beautiful day. One of those soft, warm, cloudless, slightly breezy, late spring days that make the soul smile. It was a pleasant, sun-filled and laugh-filled ride up to Rye Beach. On the boat EB met many of his old classmates. EB told them he was glad to see they were still alive. They laughed together and told Christian Brother war stories. And laughed their way up the river into Long Island Sound.

He also met one of his old girlfriends, Maggie Molloy.

She was another sight to make the soul smile.

He saw her across the deck, standing in a crowd of McAuley girls, caught her eye, and waved. She waved back with enthusiasm.

Promising.

Of course, meeting Maggie was no accident. He knew she would be on the boat ride and he was hoping. Always hoping. He loved her dearly, in his own EB kind of way. Their on-again, off-again romance extended back to grammar school, but he hadn't seen her in over a year.

But today he was hoping.

He didn't see her again after the boat docked and the happy and exhilarated mixed crowd of Augustine and McAuley kids spread out through the amusement park.

EB, Red Wallace, and a few of their friends spent the day enjoying the rides, the attractions, the games, and the food. They managed to sneak in a few beers, but they were careful; it was not that kind of day and it would be unseemly to be caught by one of the brothers.

Playland had an old wooden roller coaster that was a bit of a killer. It wasn't that high, it didn't have that dramatic, gut-wrenching first drop of the Cyclone in Coney Island, but it was sneaky fast and unexpectedly twisty. And it was old...really old...so that added to the sense of adventure. You got the impression that the whole thing could collapse at any moment. It was fun. EB and Red Wallace loved it and rode it a half dozen times on that fine day.

Around three o'clock in the afternoon, they were all moving toward the dock preparing to board the boat for the trip back to New York City. EB and Red had stopped at the game tents and EB was firing a .22 rifle at lighted candles trying to extinguish the flame and win a prize.

Not in this lifetime.

Maggie Molloy suddenly appeared at his side with a big smile, put her hand on his shoulder, and made a joke about his shooting prowess. She was there and that puffed him up, and he concentrated hard to snuff out that candle flame.

Not in this lifetime.

But she was there and showing every sign of wanting to stay. And that was the biggest prize of the day. They stayed together for the boat ride back to the city in a mixed group of their friends. The conversation was light and kidding. Casual. At the dock, Red Wallace, Maggie, and EB walked over to the Broadway IRT and took the subway back to Brooklyn. Red got off at Newkirk Avenue, God bless him, and EB and Maggie stayed on the train to the next and final stop, Flatbush Avenue.

In twenty minutes they were sitting together in the back room of Grote's sipping a beer and talking quietly. It was early evening and they stayed until just before midnight. Quietly. Talking. Just talking.

The conversation covered a lot of ground and it was very personal, if not intimate. They had known each other for a long time, but that night they talked of things they had never discussed before. They talked about their fathers, both of whom were alcoholics. They spoke openly and honestly and emotionally. Maggie was misty-eyed when she described the "troubles" in the Molloy home. EB, of course, could understand, empathize, and match her experience for experience. Drunks, it seemed, were drunks no matter where they lived or who they hurt.

That night he walked her home. At her door he kissed her softly, tenderly. Then he looked deep into her eyes and kissed her again, long and hard. And then asked if he could see her again.

Yes.

So they were an item again. Sort of. With EB, it was always sort of. He was still the same uncomfortable suitor, unwilling or unable to commit himself first. This girl would never know how much he cared for her.

But for now, they were on again. Sort of.

At the end of May, Jerry Frost and Jimmy Ready were home on boot leave. That meant another two weeks of celebration. EB was getting worn down. Celebration was hard on the body and the mind.

Jerry's father threw him a small party on the first Saturday night in June. EB asked Maggie to go with him. Not everybody had a date that night, but EB was running out of Saturday nights and did not want to waste one without Maggie. It was a wonderful party. Intimate. A few old friends enjoying each other's company after months of absence. Jimmy Ready was there, Billy Janson and Bobby Waegelein were there with dates. Maggie fit right into this group. All of the girls and all of the boys had known her as long as EB had. It was a good night. A comfortable night. A memorable night.

The party ended early, before twelve, and moved to McDade's. No way EB would take Maggie Molloy into McDade's, so he and she drifted away. They got as far as a darkened doorway around the corner and necked for an hour or so. He loved kissing her. He was thrilled to kiss her. As they warmed to the task, he wanted more. He longed to touch her, just touch her. He ached to touch her, but he couldn't. He was afraid to offend her. He didn't know. To him it was unthinkable that she wouldn't be offended...that she wanted him to touch her...that she felt the same as he did. Unthinkable. He just didn't know.

The nuns did their job well.

The nuns did him in.

The boot camp warriors returned to the Navy, and EB's other life returned to normal. The semester was almost over, and as far as he could tell, everything was OK at Midwood. He would graduate in a week.

Not so fast, Mr. Wiseguy.

On Friday, June 20th, EB was called down to the principal's office. The man had a sad, disappointed look on his face. EB stopped dead in his tracks. And waited. He was told that he had passed all his subjects except one, and that meant that he could not be graduated.

The subject was music.

EB stood there in shock, more severe shock than he felt when he broke his ankle...YOU STUPID BASTARD...YOU WISEASS JERK...he said to himself. He looked at the principal and said...IT'S MY FAULT...I LET THE TEACHER DOWN...I DID NOT FULFILL MY COMMITMENT TO HER...I FEEL TERRIBLE...I'M SORRY...I'M DESPERATE...CAN I SPEAK TO HER?...the principal was now an EB fan (why that was so EB did not spend the time to figure out...maybe it was his father's visit to the school) and told him that he would allow it, and if EB could work it out with the teacher, then it was still possible that he could graduate on time.

Still alive.

EB rushed upstairs to the music room. For one of the few times in his life, he felt like crying...WHAT A SHITHEAD! HOW COULD YOU BE SO STUPID! ASSHOLE!

She was in the middle of a class and EB had no choice, he had to knock on the door and ask her to come out. She did. And he poured his heart and soul into it. His eyes were misty...PLEASE FORGIVE ME...IT'S MY FAULT...I FORGOT...I MEANT TO DO IT...BUT I FORGOT...THAT'S THE TRUTH...I WAS GRATEFUL TO YOU FOR TREATING ME WITH RESPECT...AND NOW I'VE TURNED AROUND AND TREATED YOU WITH DISRESPECT...I'M SO SORRY...I FEEL TERRIBLE...BUT PLEASE...PLEASE, GIVE ME ANOTHER CHANCE...I'M DESPERATE...I'M GOING INTO THE NAVY IN SIX DAYS...I HAVE NO TIME LEFT...PLEASE ALLOW ME TO WRITE THE ESSAY OVER THE WEEKEND...AND I'LL HAVE IT IN YOUR HANDS ON MONDAY MORNING... PLEASE...HELP ME.

She agreed. Angel. Saint.

EB hurried to the library and dove into the subject of music. He read and read and scanned and scanned. In the end, he wrote about what he knew best. Popular music...from Crosby, Sinatra, Como, and Dick Haymes to Guy Mitchell and Johnny

200

Ray. From Mildred Bailey, Ella Fitzgerald and Billie Holiday to Kay Starr, Patti Page and Joni James. From the age of the big bands to the emergence of the singer as king and queen. And how all of this was a reflection of the society in which it existed. And how music and lyric evolve not in sync with the changes in society but in advance of it.

Predicting it.

And precipitating it.

Both observer and catalyst.

That was the sense of EB's essay. He began working on it in the Midwood library on Friday afternoon and finished it at home on Sunday night. He delivered it on Monday morning, June 23rd, as promised.

The young music teacher...the pretty young music teacher...the angelic young music teacher...read the essay that morning and graded it with a 90%. She reported that to the principal who, in turn, called EB down to the office and informed him that he now had a 90 to go with his 65s. And to give him the joyful news that he was graduated.

Whew!

Take the rest of the week off, EB.

It was hot in the final weeks of June 1952. Torrid. It hit 96 degrees on Tuesday the 24th. And it was a Brooklyn 96, which means it was matched with a 96 percent humidity. It was so humid that EB's clothes were sticking to his body. It was so hot that Glenwood Road was sticking to his shoes.

On Tuesday afternoon, EB was sitting in Pease's saying his last good-byes to whoever was still around. At one point, he was sitting in the back of the candy store holding a can of soda. He held it low, under his face, in just the right spot so that the sweat dripping off the end of his nose hit the top of the can with a semi-musical PING...PING...PING...PING.

Early that evening, he invited Bud Bohan for a few farewell beers in Grote's (Buddy was still a tad too young to drink in McDade's). EB made him promise to take care of East 40th Street in his absence. He kidded Buddy that he was still his agent and when he came back he wanted to be a famous ball player and a fabulously popular singer. Buddy smiled and, possessing a fine sense of humor, said he'd work on it.

After a while, they were joined by Eddie Mitchell and Jack Noonan. Eddie was soon to be a Marine along with Jake Teahan.

Eddie Mitchell...a Marine. A good and proud Marine.

A stranger thing never happened.

Jack Noonan, on the other hand, would join the Army and spend his tour of duty in the trenches in Chicago. Tough duty! Jack was a tall kid, about six-two or three, and even then you could see the banker he would become. He was fussy, precise, literal, and conservative in bearing. And like all those cliché bankers in the old black and white movies, Jack did not suffer fools gladly. But, again like the bankers in the old movies, once you got past the rather gruff exterior you found a generous, empathetic soul with an active sense of humor and a kind, and giving heart. Still, you had to dig to get there. Which is why Buddy Bohan claimed that Jack was his own worst enemy because he seemed old before his time. And at that point, even though Jack was not yet seventeen, Buddy began calling him "the Oldtimer".

And naturally, it stuck.

So, on this night, the night before EB's last night at home, he and his friends had a quiet little farewell celebration in Grote's Bar and Grill, Brooklyn, New York.

The biggest small town in America.

EB left them early, around 9PM, to make his way up to Avenue D to say farewell to Maggie Molloy. He called for her at the house and said his good-byes to her mother, then he and Maggie went for a walk.

It was still very hot, not much below ninety, even at this hour of the night. They walked the few blocks to Paerdegat Park and sat on one of the benches in the quiet northern end of the park. They hugged and kissed, and snuggled and talked, and kissed and snuggled. She cried and sobbed. So did he. But only on the inside.

Around midnight he walked her home.

At her door, they stopped and embraced. And waited. It was an awkward moment for both of them. EB was completely off balance. He didn't have a clue how to handle this moment. He wanted to ask her to wait for him. But he knew that was totally unfair. He would be gone for three years, the best three years of her young life. So it was out of the question. But he wanted to ask her anyway. He thought he had to at least bring it up. He could not just say goodnight and walk away for three years.

If he didn't ask, she would be hurt, he figured. He didn't know. He wasn't sure. But finally he decided get it out, to face it head-on as he always did, to bring out what they both knew was hanging there in the air between them. But he knew he could get hurt here. He would be leaving himself wide open for a serious ego blow.

He didn't like those.

He had to protect himself.

So he asked the question in the EB way...in negative form so it would seem as if he already knew the answer...I DON'T SUPPOSE IT WOULD BE FAIR FOR ME TO ASK YOU TO WAIT FOR ME WOULD IT?...he whispered. She looked up at him through misty eyes, but those lips that he had been loving and kissing for hours did not make a move.

They didn't have to.

Her eyes said it all. Please don't ask me to do that, they said. I'm too young. Three years is too long, they said. Please don't ask me to wait.

So he didn't.

And she didn't.

21

Chapter Twenty-One-Leaving

On the morning of EB's last day, his mother made an unusual and aggressive speech. She insisted that he stay close to home. In other words, EB, you're grounded. OK, he had no plans to do anything other than that anyway.

Then his mom asked him what he would like for his farewell dinner. She said he could have anything he liked... WOULD YOU CARE FOR A STEAK?...SIRLOIN?, PERHAPS?... PORTERHOUSE?...HOW ABOUT ROAST BEEF AND BAKED POTATO?...POT ROAST?...OR SOMETHING MORE EXOTIC?... YOU CAN HAVE ANYTHING YOU WANT...ANYTHING...his mother finished.

And waited.

FRICADELLER...EB said.

FRICADELLER?...his mother asked. She was surprised.

Shocked even... FRICADELLER!...THAT'S THE LAST THING I EXPECTED YOU TO SAY...IF YOU'RE WORRIED ABOUT THE MONEY DON'T BE...she said...WE CAN AFFORD A COUPLE OF STEAKS, F'GOODNESS SAKES.

A fricadeller was basically a hamburger...with a twist. It was his mom's grandmother's semi-secret recipe passed down from Germany. It was part beef and part pork (the proportion was the secret part), and cooked well so that it was really crispy on the outside, and EB loved the crunchy texture and the unexpected pork/beef taste of it. It was usually served with mashed potatoes and French-cut string beans. And for a last meal, that was fine for him. He always said he was a man of simple needs.

Which, of course, was a poor kid's conceit.

His mother looked at him, saw he was serious, and told him that if that's what he wanted, then that's what it would be, and she would make the best fricadellers he had ever tasted.

So it was decided; the family would dine on the less-than-elegant fricadeller that evening.

On his last day, EB was filled with conflicting emotions. He was excited, exhilarated, and just a little apprehensive. He wasn't doubting himself, he almost never did that, but it was natural to be a little intimidated by a life-style change of this magnitude. This was the biggest thing he had ever attempted, the biggest commitment he had ever made. He couldn't wait to go, but yet he didn't want to go. This would be his very first extended stay away from home. And extended is the right word, he mused. Yes, you could fairly describe a three-year absence as extended. Yes, that was fair, he sniffed to himself. But it could be worse; he could be going in for four years like Jerry Frost and Jimmy Ready.

In the '50s, the U.S. Navy had a policy that was unique among the services. If a kid went in before he was eighteen, he was discharged before he was twenty-one. Obviously, the closer to your eighteenth birthday that you entered the Navy, the less actual time you served. EB would be eighteen in four days. You couldn't cut it any closer than that, he smiled to himself.

Beat the system again, he crowed in his head.

In retrospect, the accident and the fractured ankle were Heaven sent. (One of the best breaks he ever got...yeah, yeah,

yeah.) Because of the in-before-eighteen, out-before-twenty-one rule, he had lost no time as far as the Navy was concerned. He would go in five months later and get out at the same time. So, in one way of thinking (his way of thinking), his graduation was courtesy of the U.S. Navy. Thank you, Navy.

And thank you again, Guardian Angel.

After breakfast on that last day, he didn't quite know what to do with himself. He was restless, keyed up, but he had no immediate outlet. There was nothing left to do. His affairs were in order...which was easy to accomplish because basically he had no affairs. His good-byes were taken care of as much as possible. As far as he could tell, there were no loose ends.

Everything was done.

He was ready.

There was nothing left to do. And he had a day to kill. Finally, he told his mom he was going out for a walk and left the house. He took a right and walked down East 40th Street to Farragut Road and crossed the street and entered Paerdegat Park. It was another very hot day, almost ninety degrees, and it was still only ten o'clock in the morning. EB walked over and sat on a bench along the first base line of the softball field. There was a soft breeze and, as hot as it actually was, it did not feel all that uncomfortable.

He sat there and gazed out over the field. He laughed to himself when he remembered how much he and his very young friends hated the idea of this park when it was first being built. And how their pathetic attempts at sabotage had absolutely no effect. It was a good thing, too, he thought, because the park turned out to be a terrific addition to the neighborhood. He thought about the thousands of hours he spent there. He realized at that moment that he had probably spent more time in that park than he did at home, at school or at church. And, in a metaphoric sense, the park was a combination of all three of those important institutions in his life. The park was where he lived every day after three o'clock and all day long on weekends and a good part of every day during the summer months. The park was where he developed and polished his athletic skills, where he learned how to compete, how to give and take, how to win and how to lose. And how to accept both of those finalities with a maximum of style and a minimum of crying.

No crying, please. Not in this neighborhood.

Want to be a crybaby? Move.

And in that same metaphorical sense, the park was a cathedral. It was the temple where the older god-athletes performed and thus was a place of worship for kids like EB. And miracles really did happen in this shrine of sports worship. He remembered the spectacular plays he had seen the older guys make on Sunday afternoons in the semi-professional, windmill softball league games. He remembered Mimmie the Mooch, the greatest shortstop he had ever seen, playing shallow and handling everything on the short hop, as if it were the easiest thing in the world (it wasn't). He thought of Frank "The Dasher" Dursi blurring down the first base line faster than any human being should be allowed to go. He remembered with awe the day Don McMahon made a throw from deepest center field that looked as if it was fired from a rocket launcher. But it wasn't a rocket launcher or a cannon; it was only McMahon's right arm which, come to think of it, was a cannon. The ball came out of his hand about three feet off the ground and never dipped, died, or wavered for three hundred feet until it smacked into the catcher's glove and nailed the runner by ten feet. When Don McMahon left the neighborhood a few years later, he became a major league pitcher.

Naturally.

What else would you become if you had a cannon instead of an arm hanging on your right side?

EB reminisced about a few of his own plays and experiences. He thought about plays long forgotten by everyone else. But he remembered.

He thought about the time he was playing shortstop and on a low outside pitch moved toward the bag anticipating that the batter would hit the pitch up the middle. But the batter somehow pulled that pitch and hit a screaming low, line-drive into the hole he had just vacated. EB somehow reversed the direction of his body in mid-stride, did a split, reached back, and backhanded the ball not inches off the ground.

He had no idea how he did that.

He regarded that as a miracle.

Not a miracle that would be recognized by the Vatican,

maybe, but a miracle nevertheless.

He looked out at the twenty-foot high chain link barrier that was the right field fence. He remembered a shot he hit out there during an important game. But it wasn't just a double off the right center field fence that made it memorable for him. He hit that fence often enough. No, this was a SHOT. His swing was so perfectly timed, the pitch was so perfectly placed, so much in his wheelhouse, that the ball took off from his bat with the speed of light. It was a rising line drive that ricocheted off one of the steel support beams with a CLANG! But the amazing thing was it got there instantly, even before he finished his follow-through. A laser beam. CLANG!...it even sounded impressive. He almost stood there and admired it, but you could never do that. That was not classy. That was anti-code.

He never forgot it because he could not understand how he did it. He was not Mickey Mantle. That was the hardest he ever hit a ball in his life.

He had never done it before.

He never did it again.

It was another one of those pagan sports miracles.

And speaking of sports miracles...thought EB...how about hanging suspended in mid-air on the basketball court...just hanging there, floating longer than the rules of gravity allowed. Anybody who has ever played basketball knows this feeling. He sat there on the park bench, visualized going up for a shot, floating in space, the defender is there, in his face, so he continues to float, waiting for the other guy to go back down to earth, obeying gravity's rules while EB scoffs at them. He could feel the feeling right there, sitting on that bench. He sat there and wondered about it. Somehow, mysteriously, you stayed up there, suspended, floating. When the defense fell away and you didn't, you took the shot.

How? He had no clue. But he knew it wasn't just a feeling or a myth. He knew it really happened. Everbody knew it. But no one knew how.

Now that miracle must have been truly pagan.

The devil's work.

It was to be a day marked by nostalgia. He accepted it. It was his mood and it was not to be denied. It was a day to contemplate the future and the past. His life was changing. His neighborhood was changing. His world was changing. Hell, Bob Campbell was married now, married to the fabulous Ruth Janson, sister of EB's good friend, the moon-meister Bill Janson (how about that for a small world!). And John Campbell was married, too, to the beautiful Loretta Holleran. And both Bob and John had already had their first child.

Yes, everything was changing.

He left the park and walked down Farragut Road on the north side of the street. He passed the Byrnes' house on the corner of 40th Street. That house used to be the entrance to the "woods". But in 1952, the "woods" was long gone. That thought saddened him. His Sherwood Forest. Gone.

What a wondrous anachronism it was. Why couldn't they see the magic? Why couldn't they leave it alone?

Never mind, he knew why.

He passed 39th Street and noted Billy McLoone's house across the street. Billy and his twin sister Mary were EB's classmates at St. Vincent Ferrer. And there was Dick Duckett's house on 38th Street. And on East 37th, Bobby Waegelein's house, with Jerry Frost's house directly across the street. Now he was passing Jimmy Dillon's house on Farragut Road. And there was Billy Neugabaugh's house across the street. Jimmy played third base to EB's second base on the St. Vincent Ferrer baseball team. Billy Neugebaugh was the star pitcher on that team.

And on each of the numbered streets, there were dozens of houses of other kids he had known most of his life. On those streets, the permanence, the cohesion of it all was taken for granted. To those people, it was not seen as very noteworthy or unusual. But it was. In retrospect, it was what marked this time as special. It was the continuity, the strength of stability, and the unifying love of community that made the Brooklyn of the '40s and '50s the magical place it truly was.

EB had reached the corner of Farragut Road and Brooklyn Avenue. On his right was his mother's favorite house. It always struck EB as a house that was out of place. The house was a bastardized Spanish design with white stucco walls and arches and a distinctive red tiled roof. It was the roof that seemed wrong to EB. To him, its distinctiveness was a reach. It just didn't belong.

But his mother liked it. And that was enough for him. He never once mentioned to his mom his serious reservations about the compatibility of Spanish red tiled roofs and the borough of Brooklyn.

He crossed the street and walked up Brooklyn Avenue, continuing his nostalgic tour of the neighborhood. He knew he was wallowing in it, but it was that kind of day, he was in that kind of mood, and he was enjoying the pensive, melancholic mopiness of it. Hey, he had enough Irish blood in him to recognize the spiritual beauty of the blues.

He reached Glenwood Road and turned left. He walked down to 37th Street and crossed the street. Now he was standing in front of the front entrance of St. Vincent Ferrer church. His church. His school. His universe when he was younger.

His universe...it occurred to him then that for him there were two universes. One was the star-filled universe that belonged to everybody. The big one, the one that was up there, out there, mysterious, unfathomable, unknowable. The other was here, his neighborhood, his parish, the universe that he knew so well. The universe that belonged only to a small group of very lucky people, people who could live their whole lives in this symmetrical and safe miniature universe and seemingly never notice the other one. Never give a thought to the other one. And, of course, many people did exactly that.

But not EB. Tomorrow he was leaving his terrestrial cocoon and moving into the cosmos.

He entered the church through the massive bronze door on 37th Street, (in the '40s and '50s it was always open), walked up to the altar rail, and lit a candle in front of the Blessed Mother's altar. He prayed there for a few minutes. Not for himself, but for his mother and sister, and especially for his father. His father's drinking was the thing he worried about most of all. He knew he himself would be fine; he would handle the Navy like he handled everything in his life. He was supremely confident in his own abilities. He had proven himself over and over again to the one person who mattered most...himself.

So he knew the Navy would not be a problem.

He prayed that his father would not be a problem for his mother and sister. Please, God, protect them from his other father...the ugly father...the Mr. Hyde father.

When he finished praying, he went home.

His sister came home from school about four o'clock. EB, his sister, and their mother sat in the very hot kitchen and talked for an hour or so. Never once mentioning the anxiety they all felt. Would he come home on time? Would he be sober? Would he ruin this night, of all nights?

Please, God.

At almost exactly five forty-five, EB's father opened the front door.

Whew! Tonight it was Dr. Jekyll.

Thank you, God.

And especially...thank you, dad.

The fricadellers were a wonderful treat. The best ever, as promised. They ate in the dining room, where all important meals were eaten. And this was certainly an important, memorable, and bittersweet meal for the family, although they kept the conversation light and focused on the positive aspects of EB's upcoming adventure. They wondered where he would go, what he would see. Would he be stationed on a ship? In the Sixth Fleet? (the East Coast)...or the Seventh Fleet? (the West Coast). Or would he be land-based? EB told them that he was going to be a radioman, with the three bolts of lightening on his left arm, and that he would be stationed in Washington D.C. He really didn't believe that, of course, but he said it because to his sister and mom it meant that he could come home for weekend liberties.

And then the whole idea wouldn't seem so bad.

Or so long.

At the end of the meal, his mom left the room and returned with a card and a farewell gift. As she handed both to him across the table, she started to cry. His sister was crying, too. He read the card first and, as he began opening the small wrapped package, he starting choking a little himself. He really did not expect this. He just hadn't thought about a gift. But it made him feel good. When he opened the small box, he was surprised.

He was touched. His eyes filled.

It was a watch.

A watch with a round, black face. It had white hour and

minute hands and a sweeping red second hand; it had tiny red numerals positioned around the periphery indicating the seconds in five-second intervals; it had a steel expanding watch band... THE HANDS AND THE NUMBERS GLOW IN THE DARK...his mother said...SO YOU CAN SEE THE TIME WHEN YOU'RE STANDING WATCH IN THE MIDDLE OF THE NIGHT, IN THE DARK...his mom continued, tearfully. Lieutenant Commander Bob Campbell's input was evident here, thought EB. Or maybe his father's. His father certainly knew something about standing watch in the dark in strange and exotic places.

EB slipped the watch onto his left wrist.

He was profoundly moved. His eyes were tearing.

This was his first watch.

He was four days short of his eighteenth birthday, and he had never owned a watch in his whole life.

It wasn't a Rolex. It wasn't even an Elgin.

But it was his new watch, his very first watch ever, and it was the best they could do.

And he loved it.

And he wore it every day for three years, even when he was in places where he could have picked up a Rolex or an Omega at a bargain price.

They stayed around the dining room table talking until bedtime. Dorothy embraced him and said she would see him in the morning before she left for school. EB had to report to 39 Whitehall Street in downtown New York City at nine o'clock in the morning, which meant that he had to leave the house at eight. His father put his arm around his shoulders and told him that he would not have enough time in the morning (his father was up at five and out by six) to talk to him about "certain things", so he promised EB that he would meet him at Whitehall Street at lunch time. EB suspected that "certain things" meant a talk on sex. Something he and his father had never really discussed. A sex talk was something that Catholic fathers did not do well. He knew the talk would be awkward and probably embarrassing, but it was the thought that counted, he said to himself. He was pleased that his father wanted to talk to him about something so intimate and looked forward to it. Just seeing his dad would make him feel better he was sure.

The next morning, EB had a good breakfast with Dorothy and his mom. Dorothy left before him, and the leaving was very emotional. When she left, he was a wreck.

And he still had the farewell with his mom to go.

War would be easier than this, he thought.

He prepared to leave. He was told to travel light. Take nothing more than the clothes on your back, he was told. Leave most of your money home, they said. You won't need it.

It was another sweltering hot day. EB dressed in a short sleeve light blue shirt, dark blue slacks, blue socks, and black loafers (all of which would be sent back to his home in a few days). He had no more than twenty-five dollars in his pocket. To him that was a wad.

He went to give his mother a final embrace, but she stopped him and said she wanted to walk him around the corner to the bus.

Whoops.

He hadn't counted on this. Your mother walking you to the bus? In Brooklyn? On any other day, he would have said no chance mom, but not today. So they walked around the corner together. She was silent as they walked. He snuck a peek at his new watch three or four times as they walked. They reached Pease's candy store and stood waiting for the bus.

Danny Gordon, the surviving member of the partnership that bought the store from Mr. Pease, came out and walked up to them. He held out his hand and EB took it. They shook hands as Danny wished him good luck.

That was nice, EB thought to himself.

Across the street, the druggist came out of Dubin's and waved good-bye to him. EB waved and smiled in appreciation.

Two storefronts down from Dubin's was Vick's grocery store, where EB had worked in the fall of 1951. Vick himself came out of the door and didn't stop. He trotted across Glenwood Road, embraced EB, handed him three packs of Marlboros, and wished him well. Vick walked back across the street and stood under the awning in front of his little store. And watched the scene, saddened by the emotion of it.

As well he should have been.

Another one...another kid leaving the neighborhood. To face what? Who the hell knew? It was the damnedest non-war most Americans had ever heard of. A police action! What the hell is that? Is it a war or isn't it? And if it isn't, why the hell were they taking all these kids out of their neighborhoods? And it wasn't just any kids they were taking...they were very selective...they were taking the best of them.

These kids were very special, a unique generation. The first post-World War II generation. History has put them down as "the Eisenhower Generation" and described them as quiescent, passive, inert, vegetating.

Baloney.

Yes, they were good kids, respectful kids, but kids with an edge. Iconoclasts before it became fashionable. They would not blindly follow. They would challenge authority. They would ask questions and expect answers that made sense. But they would do it with a sense of humor.

With a sense of the game.

They would not assault authority with the venom of the generation that would follow them.

They would not have the hate of the "love generation".

They would not say "peace" when they meant "war".

They would not call a fist a flower.

Euphemism was not their style. Their approach was direct and honest but not destructive. They would not attempt to tear down the establishment. But they would tweak the system. That was their duty. That was their code. They were honor-bound to prod and poke and explore and exploit the system when they uncovered the weaknesses and the irrationalities. They instinctively knew that all systems were rife with rules that were there only because they were always there. "That's the way it's always been done" was no longer an acceptable reason. Only suckers obeyed the system when the system itself was the problem.

EB himself was a tough city kid with a well-developed urban antennae...hyper-tuned to pick up any phoniness or cheap shit or out-moded rules that could affect him and what he wanted to do. Or didn't want to do. He was a Brooklyn kid used to making his own rules.

And he did not suffer fools gladly. (An aspect of his persona that would haunt and hurt him for the rest of his life.)

He was also, like most people, a bundle of contradictions.

He was a needling, ball-busting clubhouse lawyer with a saving sense of irony and humor.

He was a street-smart wiseguy with a respectful parochial school overlay.

He was a con artist mitigated by a Catholic naiveté.

And, because he was a child of the '40s and '50s, he was a moralizer with a highly developed sense of right and wrong. Like Jack Armstrong, Superman, The Green Lantern, Captain Midnight, and the Shadow, he was a defender of liberty, justice, and the American way.

The individual was king and the institution was crud.

"Vox populi, vox deo," as Thomas Jefferson said.

"The voice of the people is the voice of God."

EB believed it. EB lived it.

Up the organization.

And please, don't give him any of your bull shit.

He was only one man (kid), but he had the multiplying strength of his convictions. In his head, he was always a crowd.

Strong, quietly confident, he was ready for the Navy. But the real question was...was the Navy ready for him?

Too late, here comes the bus.

The bus pulled around from Albany Avenue and stopped in front of Pease's. EB gave a final wave to Vick and Barney the druggist and turned and waved to Danny Gordon. Then he embraced his mother. Hard. He picked her off her feet, whirled her around in a semicircle, and kissed her cheeks as the tears flowed. He put her down tenderly, turned and boarded the bus, the steel bracelet of his very first brand new watch glinting in the sun as he reached for the hand rail.

And he was gone.

Epilogue

On the very first day, the Navy takes everything away from you. Your underwear, your clothes, your shoes, your hair, your privacy, and your individuality.

Then it gives you back a lot of Navy stuff.

Navy underwear, socks, shoes, pants, shirts, blankets, mattress covers, pillow cases, and towels. Blue Navy uniforms, white Navy uniforms, dungaree Navy uniforms, and white and blue Navy hats. And Navy rules, regulations, and orders. Strict and inviolate.

The Navy does this to make you the same as everyone else.

Then the Navy gives you three days of tests to measure the differences between you and everyone else.

The tests were called GCT tests.

They were multiple-choice, general intelligence tests that were grueling and long, and very, very comprehensive. Covering general IQ, vocabulary, math, mechanical aptitude, and anything and everything.

The highest mark you could get in the general intelligence test was 77.

Most of the recruits scored around 30 to 40.

The brighter kids scored in the 50s.

Most of EB's friends scored from the mid to the high 60s. EB's score was 70.

The test results were posted on the bulletin board on the "quarterdeck," which was the forward space on each "deck" of the barracks. The barracks were two-deck-high buildings with two companies on each deck. Each company comprised about fifty-five recruits. So on EB's deck, the test results list contained about a hundred and ten names.

EB's name was on the very top.

And it attracted a lot of attention, most of it unwanted as far as EB was concerned. His company commander told him that he had scored well within the top 1% of all those who had ever taken the test. And that covered a lot of years and a lot of people, he said.

Thank you, Sister Theresa Marie.

Of course EB was secretly very pleased with himself. He loved to compete and loved to win even more. But the exceptionally high score was more important because of its timing. He needed the ego boost. After his disastrous high school experiences, he needed the reassurance of knowing he was still a reasonably intelligent person. The test scores validated that and told him two other very important things as well:

1) he was still the world's greatest test taker;
2) and high school hadn't ruined his brain.

Soon after the GCT test scores were posted, a guy named Myers came looking for EB. When he found him, EB was sitting on a bunk bed talking to another "boot." Myers stood in front of him with a more than slightly astonished look on his face...YOU'RE HIM?...YOU'RE THE GUY ON THE HEAD OF THE LIST?...he asked incredulously...YOU'RE THE GUY WHO SCORED A 70?...he was evidently having a difficult time reconciling EB's look with EB's score. Maybe because EB still looked to be around twelve years old.

It turned out that Myers was a college graduate (the company's one and only) and the oldest guy in the whole damn barracks. He had scored a 66 on the test and was slightly pissed that this kid, who looked like he should still be in grammar school, outscored him.

Tough shit, thought EB, who was slightly offended by Myers' reaction to his less-than-grizzled physical appearance... COLLEGE IS A WASTE OF MONEY, ANYWAY...was the most outrageous thing he could think of to say to Myers...ANYTHING WORTH LEARNING YOU LEARN IN GRAMMAR SCHOOL...he continued and would have gone on from there, but Myers walked away, shaking his head.

So you would expect with a score like that EB could have any job he wanted in the Navy, right?

A 70...wow...name your ticket, kid.

WELL, I'D LIKE TO BE A RADIOMAN...said EB in his boot camp interview, which was simply a duplication of his Brooklyn recruiting office interview. Even the yeoman looked the same...AND GO TO SCHOOL IN WASHINGTON, D.C....he concluded.

Mmmm, said the Navy.

Did they make him a radioman?

Of course not.

That's not the way the Navy works.

They looked at that 70 score in the intelligence test, they factored in the fact that this kid was born in Brooklyn, and added to the equation the probability that this kid was a wiseguy, bright but an independent thinker, a possible pain in the ass like the rest of those Brooklyn guys, and a potential danger to the system. The Navy added up all those variables and reached an informed, rational Navy decision.

They made him a spy.

They made the Brooklyn wiseguy a spy.

218

The Navy stroked him, caressed him, identified him as a romantic figure (come in from the cold, EB), told him he was special in the system, important to the system, indispensable to the system. And thus seduced, he was no longer a danger to the system.

Because he was the system.

That's the way the Navy thinks. That's the way the Navy really works.

Brilliant.

Dwight Eisenhower was elected that November with the promise that he would end the Korean War.

And he did.

After a fashion. For a while there it was hard to tell.

The Korean War really didn't end.

It just ran out of time.

But the good news was that while EB and his friends were serving their country, there was no shooting war. Where there was no shooting war, there were no casualties. And that was a blessing. So in three or four years, EB and his buddies had done their duty and were discharged. All in one piece. All together again. Ready to resume their lives.

Older, wiser, and slightly more mature.

And, in EB's case, ready to seriously commit to continuing his education in college. He was ready to work hard and study hard. Which he did.

And please...do tell that to Sister Austina.